Praise for
Teach Me Sales

You don't get great at sales in a day. You get great at sales day-by-day. *Teach Me Sales* is the daily formula that puts you on the path to a lifetime of selling success. Buy it. Read it. Implement it!

—**Jeffrey Gitomer, author of *The Little Red Book of Selling***

Teach Me Sales is an engaging, entertaining and enlightening book. Tom Bloomer shares his gifts of storytelling, humor, habits, processes and encouragement to guide you to become a complete, successful salesperson. Invest five minutes a day for twenty-one days and enjoy your sales and personal growth. You can do it!

—**David Cottrell, author of *Monday Morning Leadership***
and *Quit Drifting, Lift the Fog and Get Lucky*

Teach Me Sales by Tom Bloomer is one of those books that simply makes sense. It doesn't take very long to realize he's experienced and articulate, and he knows what he's talking about when it comes to selling. Tom breaks down selling into twenty-one simple steps. Nothing fancy, nothing hard to implement... just common sense selling for today's world. I especially like the questions/to-dos at the end of each chapter. A good read whether you're new to sales or a veteran.

— **Jeff Goldberg, founder of Jeff Goldberg & Associates**

This book is a great read for anyone starting out in sales or who is already in sales and wishes they could sell more. Tom Bloomer's stories are relatable and fun to read, and his advice is excellent!

— **Katie Mullen, CEO of MMS Consulting and host of the Golden Rule of Selling podcast**

Tom Bloomer codifies the commandments for success in sales: hard work, willingness to learn and dogged persistence. Read it and practice it; it will work for you!

— **Barry Cohen, author of *10 Ways to Screw Up an Ad Campaign* and co-author of *Startup Smarts***

Tom Bloomer's book, *Teach Me Sales*, is an amazing blueprint for how professionals can become successful in the extremely competitive world of sales. In fact, the book would make a wonderful roadmap for any professional in any industry who is interested in putting themself on the map. The author breaks the book into chapters that magically create an action plan that will propel anyone to a higher level of success. Each chapter has questions designed to help the reader really dig in and understand how they approach life and how subtle changes can help them get ahead. This book is full of great examples and easy-to-remember success factoids. *Teach Me Sales* is an enjoyable, easy read, and will be a book that I recommend to my executives on a regular basis.

— **Dr. Holly A. Sullenger, CEO of Dr. Holly Speaks**

A virtual roadmap for the aspiring or seasoned sales professional, *Teach Me Sales* offers readers a "real-world" approach to what it takes to be successful in marketing and advertising sales.

— **Richard Nichols, Senior Business Account Executive at Comcast Business**

As a sales and marketing executive with over thirty years experience, I found *Teach Me Sales* to be an excellent primer for both those new to sales and for those needing a mid-career recharge. Tom Bloomer's structure and style is orderly and clear. The stories woven into the chapters bring an element of entertainment, making for a more pleasant read. *Teach Me Sales* is a roadmap for sales success and a passion builder! I would not hesitate to recommend *Teach Me Sales* to any budding or experienced sales associate.

— Patricia Wetherhold Banks, retired sales/marketing executive and current SCORE (Service Corp of Retired Executives) mentor

You don't learn to sell by simply reading a book. You have to commit to a learning process, distilling lessons along the way that you build upon as you grow. Tom Bloomer not only provides the lessons and stories that make them impactful, he suggests a pace that will make them meaningful. This book is a provocation to learn selling the right way, one day at a time.

— Jeff Bajorek, author of the *Rethink The Way You Sell* and host of The Why and The Buy podcast

Whether you're new to sales or looking for a structured process to be more successful, *Teach Me Sales* will help you! Tom Bloomer takes you on a 21-day journey. It's like he's riding along with you on sales calls for three weeks. Each day is a new lesson like "Make the first sixty seconds of every interaction count." Or "Life is change. Growth is optional. Choose!" The author has packed a ton of wisdom from his years of success in sales into a great book that's easy to digest and implement. A must-read for sellers looking to up their game!

— Jeff Goldstein, founder of SalesLeadersOnly.com

TEACH ME
SALES

TEACH ME
SALES

A 21-Day Roadmap
to Sales Success

by
TOM BLOOMER

EMERALD LAKE
BOOKS
Sherman, Connecticut

Books published by Emerald Lake Books may be ordered through your favorite booksellers or by visiting emeraldlakebooks.com.

Library of Congress Cataloging-in-Publication Data
Names: Bloomer, Tom, author.
Title: Teach me sales : a 21-day roadmap to sales success / by Tom Bloomer.
Description: Sherman, Connecticut : Emerald Lake Books, [2021] | Summary: "How long is the road to sales success? It can be a very long one if you're on the wrong path to begin with. Tom Bloomer, a sales leader with over thirty years of experience, shares insights into how to succeed in sales. His 21-day roadmap will help you build the daily habits required to not only find your path, but take the steps necessary to excel and prosper along it. Each chapter is designed to encourage you to commit to that extra degree of effort to invest in yourself and your future along this rewarding and personal journey. Day 1 begins now"-- Provided by publisher.
Identifiers: LCCN 2021020896 (print) | LCCN 2021020897 (ebook) | ISBN 9781945847462 (paperback) | ISBN 9781945847479 (epub)
Subjects: LCSH: Selling. | Success in business. | Christian life.
Classification: LCC HF5438.25 .B5677 2021 (print) | LCC HF5438.25 (ebook) | DDC 658.85--dc23
LC record available at https://lccn.loc.gov/2021020896
LC ebook record available at https://lccn.loc.gov/2021020897

Contents

Foreword

TOM BLOOMER AND I WORKED TOGETHER for seven years at Clipper Magazine, where I was CEO and he managed one of our largest regions for nearly thirty years. Tom is a strong manager and leader, and his team was always very loyal to him. This loyalty was forged over many years, thanks to the quiet, steady confidence that Tom possesses.

Sure, Tom was a great teacher, but a writer? What could he add that the countless other books on this subject missed? The truth is, the others don't possess the immersive experience that Tom's *Teach Me Sales* does. His ability to distill thirty years of on-the-street experience into actionable lessons that cross all industries is a unique experience for the reader.

I started my own sales journey working for a small CBS affiliate in rural Pennsylvania, then onto a career as a television syndicator selling television shows to local affiliates across the country, both out of New York and then Los Angeles. I have worked in sales and leadership roles at The Los Angeles Daily News, The Washington Post, The Wall Street Journal, and Gannett Co. I was fortunate to be involved with the launch of Cars.com and many other digitally focused verticals. I have worked with thousands of salespeople, including the more than five hundred I worked with at Clipper.

During my career, I have had the privilege of witnessing some truly outstanding performances that were replicated year after year. The question I always had was what makes a great salesperson a spectacular one? The answer is simple. Great salespeople can be born, but spectacular salespeople work at it. They are consistently working on their craft, searching out tools and strategies, and putting them to use in their own practice, filling the holes they have in their game. I believe this book is one of those tools.

Tom takes us on a 21-day journey that reminded me of what led to my passion for sales. Readers who utilize the many best practices Tom shares will be on their way to becoming spectacular.

While my days enjoying significant windshield time are well behind me, I will say Tom had me fondly reminiscing. Today, I work in healthcare education as the co-founder of the largest medical education company in the world. StatPearls.com offers continuing education to individual users as well as hospitals and medical schools for all healthcare professions and certification and board reviews for more than five hundred twenty medical exams. There are significant sales activities to engage in with my current industry, and Tom's lessons are just as relevant here.

I found *Teach Me Sales* not only an enjoyable and rewarding sales book, but this 21-day approach is filled with the "why" and the "how." Each chapter shows how Tom learned to find his success while inspiring the reader to apply these lessons to their own situation.

Succeeding in sales is often as much about motivation as it is about knowledge. There are features and benefits to learn, but there are also relationships and trust to be built. *Teach Me Sales* takes us through a clear process that results in understanding how it all comes together when done for the right reasons in the right way.

In just a few short days, Tom will show you how very similar he is to you. He has knocked on the doors, made the mistakes, and found ways to build and grow. He worked at his craft for thirty years, and this book covers it all, from cold calls and prospecting to presentations and follow-ups. This is not a theoretical exercise, and you will not be fooled into trying "can't miss" shortcuts. There are no shortcuts when you are learning to become spectacular. You will receive valuable instruction, not only on how to sell, but how to live a sales career you will be proud of, with an approach that will be unique to your best skills.

Each day on your journey will build on the last as you build new habits that will make you a stronger seller. Like you and I, Tom has a passion for success. His goal in *Teach Me Sales* is to help you achieve the success you are striving for.

You have taken the first step on the road to spectacular, and I wish you the best in your journey. It's going to be a great one!

— **Steve Hauber, President and CEO of StatPearls**

Let the Journey Begin

YOU HAVE PROBABLY HEARD that "The road to success is always under construction." Unfortunately for too many in sales, never-ending detours lead to dead ends and scenic routes, leaving you lost on the road to the success you desire. If that sounds familiar, you have found the right book to help you navigate your path forward.

Like so many sales professionals, you have probably ended up in your sales career without formal training. You may even be learning about sales simply by trial and error. While this method can ultimately work, it often takes far too long. Motivated and hungry sales professionals like yourself may simply run out of gas or start searching for shortcuts before reaching the elusive destination you are striving for: success.

Alternatively, you may be in a relatively good and safe place, but you haven't reached the destination you dreamt of yet. You have seen others succeed where you have not and wondered what path they found that brought them there.

Further complicating your sales efforts and growth are the many alternative routes available to you. If you have ever used a GPS to arrive at your destination you have seen the myriad options available. Unless you have already travelled these paths and are familiar with them, it can be difficult to know which route is your best choice.

Jim Stovall, successful author, athlete and entrepreneur, wrote in his book, *The Millionaire Map:*

> Never accept a map from someone who hasn't
> been where you want to go.

Like you, I have had to find my own way. I have had to choose from those many options and am able to share insights into what lies ahead for you. I have followed several detours, wrong turns, and a few seemingly dead ends. My journey, however, has included roles as a seller, sales manager, regional manager and Vice President of Sales.

I am writing this book after spending thirty years in sales and sales leadership to provide you with a roadmap that will guide you through the messy construction you face. I am uniquely qualified to guide your journey as I have walked the walk myself and been where you want to go.

I was fortunate to be blessed with a few amazing opportunities that enabled me to not only grow in my own sales career, but to develop and teach hundreds of other sales professionals to grow in their careers as well. Having experienced obstacles and detours myself, combined with a background in education and leadership, has given me the chance to help others avoid many of the most difficult detours along the way.

Having seen firsthand the impact this knowledge can have on aspiring sales reps, I became inspired to share my stories. The vast majority of sales reps I have met genuinely want to connect with their prospects and help their clients. I believe my stories can be of help to you on your journey. I look forward to sharing them with you.

As you will read in the pages of this book, I have spent years on the street selling to and learning from thousands of small business owners. I will be sharing critical lessons that will help you achieve your success on the shortest road possible. I have guided hundreds of others down this same road.

Whether you are in a sales role or you need to sell yourself or your business to others, I believe you already have the gifts inside you to achieve greatness. I promise this book will help you navigate the many routes ahead of you. It will bring out those gifts inside and help you inspire those around you. If you have ever wished for a more supportive manager, a strong mentor, or just a caring coach, this book is designed to be your co-pilot, to be the supportive passenger navigating and travelling beside you. Along with this experienced guidance, all you need is already inside you.

So how do you find your path in this ever-changing, increasingly complicated world?

This book is a collection of ideas, stories and daily motivation to help find your way as a salesperson. I know from experience that following a path is difficult enough even once you find the right road, and tremendously frustrating and unsuccessful when that road is obscured. This 21-day roadmap will help you build the habits necessary not only to find your path but take the first steps to excel and prosper along it. Since each day builds on the one before, I recommend not skipping any chapters.

I will ask a lot of you over the next twenty-one days, and you should ask even more of yourself.

William McKinley, the twenty-fifth president of the United States, once said:

> It is just as easy to form a good habit as it is a bad one. And it is just as hard to break a good habit as a bad one. So, get the good ones and keep them.

To help you "get the good ones," I will share stories from my career, showing how I consistently tried stepping outside my comfort zone and how I encouraged others to do so as well. So, I am asking you to stay tuned, stay engaged, do the little extras, and challenge yourself.

Make your first good habit that of taking daily notes. You should feel compelled to jot down a few ideas and plans as you read each day's chapter. This roadmap covers twenty-one days that require you to do the little things, give it that extra effort, and invest in yourself every day. It involves much more than simply reading these pages. Engage in them and use them to discover your path. Take your time and make this a rewarding journey. This roadmap is designed to enable you to manage yourself to sales success. Commit to reading and exploring one chapter every day for the next twenty-one days.

This journey will require you to do some reflection and make notes along the way to track what you're learning and the progress you're making. So, I recommend having your favorite note-taking tool handy while you're reading, whether that's an app, file or notebook and pen. Slow down at the Speed Bumps at the end of each chapter to reflect on the questions there. These questions provide you with personalized guidance for how to be successful in your own sales career, and I invite you to work through them to develop the habits you'll need each day.

My ever-changing path can best be summed up by the words of St. Augustine.

Pray like it all depends on God... Work like it all depends on you.

My faith has been a huge part of my journey as I grew and developed in my sales career. I know God has always been with me, guiding me, providing for me, even when I did not realize it. At the conclusion of a few of the chapters, I have included a related scripture passage that resonated with me. I hope it does for you too. However, if it's not for you, I meant no offense and invite you to skip past it.

When I was first starting out in sales, I had the amazing good fortune of finding the right career opportunity at the right time with Clipper Magazine, an American direct mail advertising publication, where I prospered and grew for over twenty-eight years. There, I worked with countless passionate, entrepreneurial-minded individuals who truly were a gift to me. I was a Regional Vice President of Sales during my last fifteen years at Clipper, actively involved in sales, management, training, inspiring, coaching and so much more. After starting at Clipper as a sales rep earning only $25,000 a year, I continually strived to grow and excel to make things happen for me and my family.

In this book, I will share with you the essential habits I learned and taught to many outstanding, high-producing sales reps and managers during my career. Over the next twenty-one days, I will teach you how to make things happen for yourself. It's up to you to apply what you're learning to create those habits that will work for you on your path.

As civil rights leader Martin Luther King, Jr., said:

> You don't have to see the whole staircase, just take the first step.

Here's the thing. You must work on your path to success every day by taking the first step, followed by the next one. Success comes from building on the accomplishments of the day before.

In my early days at Clipper, we were trying to build a company and brand, and expand into more markets nationally. I started there in the summer of 1992 and was responsible for opening, selling and producing an advertising magazine in Cherry Hill, New Jersey. My market was only the thirteenth to have been started in the company and the farthest geographically from their Lancaster home market. (Years later, they had hundreds of different editions in over twenty-two states.) Our primary goal in building a market was to produce a local magazine full of coupons and money-saving offers that had compelling value for consumers and business owners.

As a consumer, I'm sure you can appreciate how a coupon magazine with only a handful of coupons from bottom-tier restaurants and stores might compare to a magazine containing hundreds of great offers from many of the best places in town. Which magazine would you rather receive in your mailbox? Of course! To succeed in a market, we needed a beautiful magazine featuring many pages of the best offers in town.

Simple as it seems, we learned early on that almost any *good* local sales rep could sell and produce a magazine that would deliver enough coupons to publish. But finding a *great* local sales rep who could produce a magazine that consumers loved to open and keep was exceedingly difficult. As I opened markets throughout New Jersey and other states, I learned one of the biggest differences between "good" and "great" for a sales rep at Clipper was the understanding that there are no shortcuts. So many people simply never learn that to do great things, to achieve all they want, they must first do all the little things every day.

Author and former baseball player A. Lou Vickery said it best:

> Four short words sum up what has lifted most successful individuals above the crowd—"a little bit more." They did all that was expected of them and a little bit more.

I look forward to teaching you the habits that help you do "a little bit more" and stretch yourself along the way as you prepare to make things happen for you.

Many stories I share in this book come from my experiences growing from a novice seller to a sales leader while working in direct mail advertising. I spent most of my days in door-to-door, business-to-business sales, which is where I learned how to overcome rejection while growing strong sales habits.

While your sales career will involve different stories, hopefully you will see that the key sales behaviors I teach will guide you, providing your own roadmap to success. I am challenging you over the next twenty-one days to do things you may have never done. Trust me: you can.

Let's get started.

Day One
Be the Steak

Any working plan for success must start with personal goal setting. I don't think a self-help book has ever been written that doesn't talk about setting goals. So, why do I still need to cover it? We all know we need to set goals, and you are probably already doing that. Finding ways to achieve your goals is what makes the difference. You know the questions you need to ask yourself. Who are you working for? Why? What are your priorities and convictions? What things are most important to you? Where do you want to be?

You'll find I describe things a little bit differently, though. My favorite meal is a good steak, and when I'm in the mood for one, there's nothing better. They may cost more and take more effort to buy and prepare right, but it's worth it every time. Now, I know some people would be perfectly content with ground beef. They'd make themselves a nice burger and be satisfied. But ground beef just can't compare to a nice steak in my book.

In sales, when I'm setting my goals and thinking about what I want to achieve, I think about that steak. What does it take to be the thing someone wants most? Perhaps for you, it's not a steak you want, but shrimp or pasta. Whatever it is, what makes it extra-special to you? How can you use what's extra-special about you to always present yourself to the fullest?

Personally, I want to *Be the Steak*. You won't find me settling for ground beef when there's something better to be had.

When you're setting your goals as a salesperson, what do you aim for? Are you going to Be the Steak or settle for ground beef?

And what do you do once you set those goals? It's not just about imagining what might be and setting sales targets, it's about taking action.

In the Disney movie *Lady and the Tramp*, it seems like Tramp has it figured out.

> There's a big hunk of world down there, with no fence around it… And beyond those distant hills, who knows what wonderful experiences. And it's all ours for the taking.

The world is there for the taking. And I'm sure, given the choice, Tramp would choose eating a good steak over ground beef. (Unless, of course, he had a perfect partner to share some delicious pasta with.)

In life, most people would prefer to Be the Steak, as in, they want to be and have the best of things. They can, but only if they apply themselves. So, what does it mean? And what does it take to Be the Steak?

Once you set your goals, you must take the path to get there. If you want to Be the Steak, you must understand that the loftier the goal is, the harder it will be to achieve. But you can get there if you work at it. You can become the Steak, rather than the ground beef, which is so much easier to settle for.

Over the years I spent with Clipper, I interviewed hundreds of sales candidates and, for many, there was always one common desire. They wanted to know if they could earn six figures.

For practically every rep I hired, I was responsible for their training and evaluations. I would be living with them through success and failure. Because of that, I found it vital to be honest in the interview process or risk reaping the heartache later. There is nothing worse than a demotivated sales rep who feels they were promised a $100,000 income but are struggling with a paycheck representing half of that based on the sales and commission levels they achieved. So, my answer was always, "Yes, a sales rep with Clipper can earn six figures. But unfortunately, most of our new hires will not work as hard as it takes to earn that."

There it is—the brutal truth. Most people simply won't work hard enough to get there. They can be given the same tools, the same training, the same management. However, they will walk a different path. Having a goal to achieve is great. Doing what it takes to achieve your goal is what makes the difference. Quite simply, most settle for being ground beef rather than taking the actions necessary to become the Steak they were meant to be.

I love the way basketball great Michael Jordan explained it:

> If you're trying to achieve, there will be roadblocks. I have had them; everybody has had them. But obstacles don't have to stop you. If you run into a wall, don't turn around and give up. Figure out how to climb it, go through it, or work around it.

Do you have the confidence needed to climb the wall blocking your path to success? To go through it? Or the confidence to pursue your goals daily and achieve them? How can you increase your confidence? Set your goals and let's work to make them happen for you. Challenge yourself to approach those goals from today on with more determination.

Focus on building your confidence every day, starting with today. While goal setting is the critical first step on your path to Be the Steak, it all comes down to having that confidence.

My first several years with Clipper were spent working in my car, going door-to-door to small mom-and-pop businesses, trying to convince them to advertise coupons in the magazine. I didn't have an appointment usually. I had to summon up the courage to walk in their door and interrupt their day, and then try to convince them to advertise with us. As you might imagine, my typical day was filled with rejection (and a few words I don't care to repeat). I would love to tell you that my goal every day was to make a sale, thereby earning the commissions to help support my family. Unfortunately, most days did not meet with success. Outside sales jobs gleefully toy with your confidence.

How did I find the level of confidence needed to excel in this environment? I learned early on that most of my sales involved a process—one that began with me simply building a rapport with a prospective client. During that process, I needed to show them that my product was the Steak of coupon books and I was the Steak of consultants—someone who could help my clients build a successful ad campaign. I gained confidence every day, not by making a sale, but because of the new relationships I'd begun. I learned those relationships would soon become strong sales as I continued to show value and build trust. On my best days, my presentations gave a strong sizzle of good things to come, and that helped build the confidence I needed.

As a young man growing up in the early '70s, I loved football and cheerleaders, and that meant being a fan of the Dallas Cowboys. As a fan back in their glory days, my favorite player was always Roger Staubach, the former Navy cadet turned Cowboy quarterback. He sums up confidence quite well.

> Confidence doesn't come out of nowhere. It's a result of something… hours and days and weeks and years of constant work and dedication.

Each of us must find a source within us for that hard work and constant dedication. For me, it began as a young boy sitting on my grandfather's front porch. My grandfather taught me a love of sports, politics and humor, and inspired me to pursue success. I never knew him when he was still working. All of my memories of him are from after he retired. He had been a glass salesperson, a veteran, a husband and the father of two girls. He had already lived many years by the time I came along, but he still greatly desired the best things in life. Many of those things had eluded him in his time. We spent countless hours together, and his influence and desire for me to achieve great heights forged some of the dreams of success that grew strong in me.

When I was promoted to VP of Sales for Clipper, telling my grandfather about it was one of my proudest moments. I knew what it meant to him and that he had helped shape me and had given me the desire and confidence to stay on my path.

Take a few minutes to think about your career goals.

- Where does your inspiration come from? Keep it in your thoughts. On many days, it will be the driving force to move you forward. Let's see where that inspiration takes you.

Few will work hard enough to succeed.

- Where do you see yourself in twenty-one days? In one year? In three years? In ten years?

The goals you are setting will be key to driving you on your road to sales success. Visualize daily activity goals as well as quarterly and annual sales expectations you have. Is there a promotion opportunity you'd like to see in the near future? How about striving for your company's President's Club?

Write about that in your notes. I hope you are setting a goal for yourself to form one new habit (a good one) every day, as you think about today's reading.

Once you have begun the habit of setting goals, you need to dedicate yourself to achieving them. Then, you are ready to find your path. The daily habits you learn from this book will get you there, but you must do the work.

Martial artist Bruce Lee once said:

> I fear not the man who has practiced 10,000 kicks once, but I fear the man who has practiced one kick 10,000 times.

Today, you are setting your goals (goals toward Being the Steak). Tomorrow and for the next twenty days, I will be sharing daily techniques for you to practice, practice, practice that will help you achieve these goals.

Before you move on, though, I'd like to share one final thought on goal setting. It's a particularly important one. Don't ever be trapped by the goals you have set. They are meant to help you along a path, but paths often change. Your goals can and should evolve. The goals I set back on Grandad's porch have changed many times over the years. The ones I set at work also changed many times, often as our corporate leadership decided to change them. Don't worry about yesterday's goals. Work to achieve the goals in front of you today. This can be key to maintaining the confidence you need.

So hopefully you have added some career goals to your notes. Watch to see how those goals evolve over the next couple of weeks. Not sure you can Be the Steak today?

Author Les Brown said in *The Power of Purpose:*

> You don't have to be great to get started, but you have to get started to be great.

Tomorrow, you will take the next step in your journey—and trust me, it is one you are absolutely ready for!

SLOW SPEED BUMP **Spend a few minutes** reflecting on these questions, then add your thoughts to your notes.

- How does your sales process "gleefully toy" with your confidence? What might you do differently now?
- Do you have an earnings or commissions goal? What measurables will get you there?
- What one "sales kick" should you practice daily?
- What new habit will you begin today?

Trust in the Lord with all your heart and lean not on your own understanding; in all your ways submit to him, and he will make your paths straight.

Proverbs 3:5–6

Day Two
That New Car Smell

HAVE YOU EVER BOUGHT A NEW CAR? While you may dread the experience, like my wife does, I have always enjoyed it and looked forward to my next car purchase. Being in sales only added to my enjoyment, as I loved watching the dance. If you have ever experienced it, I am sure you can probably guess the first step that car salesperson always wants to make. It's getting you in a car. "Would you like to take a test drive?" Of course, you would, and of course, they want you to.

For me, a test drive in a new car really starts with that new car smell—a refreshing sense of good things to come, of positivity; a promise of success and complete driving enjoyment ahead. They teach a car salesperson early on to get you in that car, knowing the new car's smell and feel will propel you into the sale they hope to make.

So, let's talk about creating your own new car smell. You have the opportunity every day to create a desire in others to take you for a "test drive," one that includes the best version of your own new car smell, which promises good things to come to the prospects who choose to become your customers. In every sales encounter, this vision gives you an opportunity to distinguish yourself from your competition.

Unlike yesterday, when I asked you to Be the Steak, today, you will focus on developing your new car smell. In other words, I want you to create your own unique test drive experience. Think about how different test drives are with vehicles like the Honda Accord, the Lexus 300, a family-sized minivan, or your favorite truck or motorcycle. How will a prospect's experience with you differ from your competition?

We each have our own unique gifts, passions and best traits. These are the ingredients of your individual new car smell. To properly consider them, take a moment to think about your past successes. (And add your ideas to your notes, please.) What comes to mind? Winning, earning, achieving, being recognized, or maybe simply being told you have done a great job at something? And what are you most passionate about? Whether it's writing songs, playing sports, knowing trivia, handling inventory at work, completing an assignment, or making your best friend feel better after a difficult day, we all have activities that make us smile.

Most often, these activities also come with a strong sense of accomplishment and with confidence in your ability to do them. If you happen to be the best person in your workplace at handling the weekly inventory, think about the traits you use to do so. Perhaps it's your attention to detail, your passion for numbers, or your desire to ensure you have the right product available for your customers. Think about the confident way you approach the task and the sense of recognition you receive for doing it so well.

Are you the person your friends and family call upon first when they have a problem or need an attentive listener to talk to? What do they see in you that makes you that first call? This is a great gift to have. My wife has an amazing amount of compassion that attracts people to her, especially people who need to talk to someone.

The habit I would like you to begin developing today, and exercising every day, is to understand your unique traits and incorporate them into more of what you regularly do. These are the characteristics that will help you build your own new car smell, which will turn every test drive with you into a successful meeting. Learning to share those best traits with your prospects will give you the confidence to become the Steak you've committed to being.

Now, let's consider some traits you may have overlooked. Did you include smiling on your list? Enthusiasm? How about humor, intellect, thoughtfulness, friendliness or compassion? If you included some of these, fantastic! You are beginning to understand some of your many gifts. If you didn't, it is probably because you are taking them for granted, which means you are missing out on how important those gifts can be in creating the new car smell that will capture your prospect's attention.

As you go through the upcoming chapters, I look forward to sharing a few stories about what I am most proud of in my life. I have been so fortunate to watch and learn from my two adult children as they have grown up. My wife and I were young parents, and we grew up alongside our kids. As many parents can attest, each child is unique, with their individual gifts.

My son has been blessed with an amazing smile and a loving, compassionate approach to life that makes everyone around him feel special. No wonder that, as he has struggled to find the best career for himself, he has seen his greatest successes and felt the most confident in the field of customer service. The key he is still learning is that this gift can provide a path for him to grow as a person and help him be his best.

On the other hand, my daughter grew up with a very driven personality. She can be laser-focused and shows great attention to detail. This has allowed her to achieve success in her schooling and her chosen career in behavioral science.

Both my children are still learning to utilize their gifts to formulate their test drives, but each will be unique and an important part of their success and happiness.

I mentioned smiling earlier and would like to focus on that now. How much energy does it take to smile? A few may argue it takes a little more energy some days than others, but I believe it takes the same energy to smile as not to smile. What message does someone convey when they are smiling? Have you ever felt frustrated and eager to complain as you approached someone, only to have those feelings evaporate when they turned to you with a welcoming smile and attitude?

The importance of smiling was something I learned while training new sales reps at Clipper. A fellow trainer, Donna Mast, taught one of my favorite lessons. She taught our inside sales team as well as telephone sales. I always enjoyed watching our trainees as she conducted an exercise, showing them the value of smiling while talking to prospects over the phone. She showed how you can feel a friendly smile from someone without seeing them and how that has an effect even over a phone line.

If you're not sure you believe that one, why not try it yourself? The next few times you are speaking to someone over the phone, try to gauge whether they are smiling and then think about how it affected you during that call.

Trying these different suggestions helps you better prepare your own test drive, which should include your best traits and passions, and the unique gifts that make you, you. People who feel good about themselves and what they are doing are far more productive, and others will take notice and want to be closer to you.

Another essential component of your new car smell is your enthusiasm. As you review your notes on your past successes, best traits and most passionate activities, I hope you are smiling, because you should realize that it's when you are experiencing these three things—successes, best traits and passions—that you are undoubtedly enthused!

Enthusiasm is what provides the energy needed to passionately approach every test drive. So, if you didn't include enthusiasm as one of your best traits, then today's chapter may very well be the most important in this book for you. Understand that to create the new car smell that gives you the confidence to reach your greatest successes, you will need to begin every day with enthusiasm and a smile. These two simple spices will help you become the perfect steak. Having these spices were instrumental during my outside selling days, and they are a crucial part of phone and virtual sales as well.

Enthusiasm provides the energy.

Rate your enthusiasm level today in your notes and compare it again in a couple of weeks to see if it's grown. Let's see if you can grow that level to where you want and need it to be.

As you work on your notes, remember to list your successes, traits and unique gifts, and then see which new ones you can add in the weeks ahead. Starting today, make a conscious effort to think about and use them more regularly in everything you do.

SLOW SPEED BUMP

Spend a few minutes reflecting on these questions, then add your thoughts to your notes.

- Recall a few of your most recent successes. What behaviors or gifts helped them happen?

- Consider how to best show or "test drive" your product or service. Are you using your best gifts? What new habit will better showcase those gifts?

- How would you rate your enthusiasm level? What would increase that for you?

- Imagine being more confident and enthusiastic in every sales encounter you have. What would it take to achieve that?

- Do you have an important sales presentation today with a new prospect? How can you show your best traits for them to see?

- If you are making a series of calls, what can you do to ensure that your personality, insights or key strengths are shown in those first crucial moments as you build a new relationship? (Of course, smile!)

We have different gifts, according to the grace
given to each of us. If your gift is prophesying, then
prophesy in accordance with your faith; if it is serving, then serve; if it is teaching, then teach; if it is to
encourage, then give encouragement; if it is giving,
then give generously; if it is to lead, do it diligently; if
it is to show mercy, do it cheerfully.

Romans 12:6–8

Day Three
Better Lucky than Good

I AM NOT SURE ANYONE has ever asked this question better than actor Clint Eastwood did, in his role as Detective Harry Callahan, at the conclusion of the 1971 movie, *Dirty Harry*. "You've got to ask yourself one question. 'Do I feel lucky?' Well, do ya, punk?" I used to ask a variation of that question during training seminars for new sales reps. At Clipper, our newest hires would hit the streets selling for eight to twelve weeks and then make the trip to our corporate offices in Lancaster, Pennsylvania, for a week of intense sales training. During one of my sessions in this class, I would ask the group, "Would you rather be lucky or good?" Which would you rather be?

In most sessions, many in the class would proudly proclaim they wanted to be good. I would then spend the next several minutes explaining why, during their first year at Clipper, they most likely wouldn't be particularly good. In fact, they would need to be lucky regularly before they might eventually be good. I would try to show them they could succeed while they developed their skills once they learned how to create their own luck—something they would surely need for a while.

I have always lived by this quote, often erroneously credited to the third president of the United States Thomas Jefferson:

> I am a great believer in luck, and I find the harder I work, the more I have of it.

I'm sure you strive to be good, but who wouldn't be open to a few lucky sales? You achieve those by working hard at creating opportunities for luck to work in your favor. If those sales have eluded you in the past or gone to others, let's work on changing that today.

Never being a patient person, I have always looked for ways to create success while paying my dues to master what I need to do. I didn't start my career at Clipper as a strong salesperson or even as someone with a passion for sales. I didn't have any natural sales ability. In fact, I got started in sales by accident. I was working as a director in a private postsecondary school, spending most of my time in education, accounting and management. When an opportunity for a sales position within that company came my way, I was committed to learn how to do the job. Some success there led me to Clipper, but I was still inexperienced and a novice in business. I was never the best dressed. I was not 6′3″, dark-haired and handsome. I talked too fast and often not too intelligently.

Despite lacking these qualities, I began my career at Clipper in the summer of 1992. I can still remember the first time my manager, Betsy DeLisle, traveled to meet me in Cherry Hill, New Jersey, to spend a day training and evaluating me. At this point, I had had a few successes and was feeling fairly satisfied with myself. But it only took a few presentations together for Betsy to pinpoint a few areas of improvement to address with me.

We had just finished a presentation for a local patio furniture dealer. When we walked outside, Betsy asked me to sit down at one of their displays. She spent the next several minutes patiently explaining all I was doing incorrectly—not the least of which was speaking too fast and too much. (I won't even mention how I backed my car into another vehicle in a parking lot later that day while leaving another brutal appointment!)

Suffice it to say, my sales skills were not fully developed at this point. It is also worth noting how lucky I was to have an experienced manager who not only quickly saw my weaknesses but cared enough to help me improve. While I was far from being a polished salesperson, what I did have was the tenacity to work hard to learn and improve every day. I spent an abundance of time in preparation and had the enthusiasm to succeed.

Motivational speaker Brian Tracy once said:

> I have found that luck is quite predictable. If you want more luck, take more chances. Be more active. Show up more often.

This is a great example of what kept me going in the beginning. I would start my day early, stay out longer than most, take a lot of chances, and knock on a lot of doors. Persistence was a constant companion of mine. There was plenty of time for me to improve, but I wouldn't have had that time if I hadn't gotten lucky first by taking more chances.

The real question for you today is, "How do you get luck on your side? How do you create the opportunity to be lucky?" Hard work and long hours would seem the easy answer.

Actually, that reminds me of an old joke:

> To be successful here you only need to work half days. That is right, simply choose which half you want to work. Would you like the first twelve hours of the day or...

Now, I'm not sure about you, but as a late twenty-something trying to enjoy life with my wife and two young children, spending twelve hard hours at work every day was not very appealing. What would you think you need to spend? Eight hours? Four hours? How many hours a day will it take to create the luck you need to become good? Thankfully, I discovered—and hope you do too—that if you master being good for the first sixty seconds, your luck will increase at making a sale.

To begin, you need to understand the importance of the first sixty seconds of every encounter you have each day. Most of us will have no more than thirty to sixty important encounters a day. These can be customer service encounters, meetings with supervisors, discussions with peers, explaining assignments to staff, or a variety of family, community, school or parental interactions. Each one begins with an opening, of which the first sixty seconds will determine how that interaction will develop—and whether you create an opportunity to have luck on your side.

In those sixty seconds, you will have an opportunity to make sure that person:

- takes you seriously
- pays attention to you
- actually considers your thoughts or proposal
- gains a desire to see and speak with you more often

Those are the four outcomes you need to succeed in your dealings with most people. And they will often be based on the first sixty seconds of your interaction. You can research plenty of articles on the significance and importance of creating a positive first impression; the key for us is learning how to master it.

It is during these first sixty seconds that you need to set yourself apart. Show how you are uniquely different from many of the other people this individual will encounter that day. Whether speaking with a supervisor, customer, prospect, future friend or someone you meet on the street, those first sixty seconds are critical. There are several things you can do to make that positive first impression that don't reduce your precious sixty seconds. You can set yourself apart by the way you dress, your grooming, your smile, your enthusiasm, and any materials you carry. Eye contact, listening skills, and an air of persistence are also important and take no time to share. If you are comfortable with polite humor, use it. If you have a strong intellect, bring it out. If you are knowledgeable about a relevant topic or product, show it. If you are creative, use your creativity to set yourself apart. These are some of your strengths, and they can be part of your brand or of the new car smell you worked on during Day Two.

Early on, I found several ways to increase my luck at Clipper. Since I wasn't a natural salesperson, I found my best approach was to go quickly to my strength, the magazine itself—the package I carried. If I was calling on a new restaurant prospect, I would have prepared six to twelve cool sample ads from other restaurants we were helping. I knew this new prospect didn't care who I was or what I could do for them, not yet. But if the

Set yourself apart in the first sixty seconds.

sample ads I showed got their attention, they would take me more seriously and hopefully agree to speak with me longer or more often. Smiling, being enthusiastic, making eye contact, going to my strength, and then asking a few relevant questions became my key to how I framed those first sixty seconds.

The next thing I needed to master was what I thought of as my packaging. I wanted to show an air of confidence without alarming my new prospect into putting up walls to ward me off. When I walked into a prospect's store, I would simply carry a few magazines rolled up and opened to the sample page I wanted to show. I carried no business card and no briefcase. I just entered their store and browsed their merchandise and displays, hoping to give a certain impression—the impression that I was a potential shopper or buyer. That would often give me the initial sixty seconds of a prospect's attention so vital to my success. They would be more excited to see me than if I were just another salesperson intruding upon their store, taking up their time and trying to sell them something. Once we made eye contact, my smile, my enthusiasm, and my habit of quickly showing my strength (those beautiful magazine ads) would get me my sixty seconds of sizzle.

In sixty seconds, there's no way to show someone you are the Steak they need to talk to or work with, the Steak that can do the job, the Steak they should buy from. No, you can't show that in sixty seconds. But the first sixty seconds aren't about being the Steak, they're about making the Steak sizzle.

This will pave the way for a more productive initial encounter, as well as for future encounters.

I would like to illustrate a subtle difference by looking at two types of encounters you may have experienced. I don't think anyone particularly enjoys waiting in line, yet we often have to do just that. Can you remember a time when the person you were waiting for was talking to another customer or employee? Or, worse yet, talking on their phone? Were you frustrated? Now, remember a time when, as you approached the counter while that employee was helping another customer (or even speaking on a phone), they glanced at you and told you they would be right with you. They acknowledged you, and even if the wait time was the same, you were considerably less frustrated. Now, picture that employee coming to wait on you with a big smile and a hello.

For those in any form of customer service, this simple act—eye contact and a quick greeting—can make a huge difference in your day and in how your customers perceive your performance. This is simply one example of the potential impact of your first sixty seconds. Never forget that your smile and enthusiasm are two important aspects of your new car smell you always want to show. Your goal is to set yourself apart. You are the new car you want them to take for a test drive.

In tomorrow's chapter, I will discuss "putting on a show." But for now, understand that in those first sixty seconds, when you have the prospect's attention, they are deciding whether to spend more time with you. If you take a minute, I am sure you can think of a recent encounter that didn't go as well as you would have liked. Reflecting back, could you have started with a different approach? Could that possibly have resulted in a better outcome? Learning how to connect with another person in those first sixty seconds can be a game-changer for creating opportunities for yourself.

There's a subtle difference in sales today from when I was knocking on doors. Far too often the first sixty seconds won't be face-to-face or even over the phone. You must create an even stronger desire to test drive a new product or service when you engage with prospects through email or direct messaging.

Apply the same gifts and ideas we've gone over already. For some, video emails and messages will be the perfect technique. For others, it may be all about including the proper links, illustrations and bullets. Be authentic and exhibit your best examples. Remember, the goal of those first few seconds, even as they read your message, is for them to take you seriously and pay attention to what you have to share.

So, would you rather be lucky or good? Is it talent or opportunity that will make you successful? If, like me, you could use a little luck to get started or while you are working hard to become good, then use your gifts and best traits to master those first sixty seconds. Do not let opportunities disappear before you can take advantage of them.

Think, smile. Think, eye contact. Think smile and eye contact until they naturally happen at the start of every new encounter.

SLOW SPEED BUMP | **Spend a few minutes** reflecting on these questions, then add your thoughts to your notes.

- What gifts should you work into your first sixty seconds?
- What are the most effective materials you can show?

- What are some thoughtful questions you may ask?
- Are there any video or internet resources you need to begin using? What are they?

Day Four
Putting on a Show

WHO SAID "WHATEVER YOU ARE, BE A GOOD ONE?" Is it crazy to think we have all said it and that we all believe it? Wouldn't it be great if you woke up every morning with the belief you would be a good one—a good father, a good mother, a good boss, a good employee, a good friend?

That is what I would like to ask you to do in this chapter. Realize how great you can be and then learn how to be noticed and make a positive impression on everyone you meet.

"Whatever you are, be a good one" is often incorrectly attributed to Abraham Lincoln. It's easy to believe he would say something like that, though. Honest Abe was the epitome of someone who built a life from nothing. He overcame poverty, the childhood loss of his mother and younger sister, and the burden of having to rely mostly on himself for much of his childhood. How did he accomplish so much in his life? He claimed:

I will **prepare** and **someday** my chance will come.

For me, that chance came when I started at Clipper. My children were still young then—my daughter was only two and my son was four. Back then, they both still needed car seats when we went out for a drive. We had only one car, a two-door Nissan Sentra with a small trunk and more duct tape than any car should need. I have told you about my strength when I began selling for Clipper, namely knowing how to use those beautiful magazine samples. Well, each morning, I would take both car seats out of the car and put them in the house, then carry my files from the house to the back seat. And every night, I would repeat the same ritual in reverse.

Preparing to have a few sample magazines worked perfectly for the first sixty seconds with a client. When those sixty seconds successfully grabbed a business owner's attention and made them want to hear more from me, it was time for the show to begin. That meant several more samples and flyers I could use for a full sales presentation of twenty to thirty minutes. Having enough sample ads to put on a show was simply more than my small trunk could manage—hence my daily ritual of moving ads in and out of the house. I had learned how important it was to have the right materials to move my sale along. Thus, I wouldn't let a lack of space prevent me from having them on hand.

Most nights after the kids fell asleep, I would pore over various issues of Clipper Magazine, looking for just the right sample ads for upcoming appointments and prospecting. Typically, an upscale jewelry store wouldn't be interested in speaking with me, and they certainly wouldn't be looking for ways to spend more money on advertising. Nurturing a sale required having just the right sample ads to get their attention and convince them to listen to more of my presentation. I could never be sure which store would listen to me or when I would finally meet the right decision maker, but I knew I had to be prepared; someday, my chance would come.

As I transitioned from sales rep to sales manager, I experienced many frustrations, including realizing how few of the reps I trained would dedicate as much time as I had to creating a full arsenal of samples. As I rode along with new reps on their prospective calls, we would inevitably get time with a strong prospect only to put on a lackluster show because we simply hadn't come prepared with the sample ads that should have been our greatest strength. What could have been an engaging, thoughtful twenty- to thirty-minute presentation (a magnificent show) would often become a lackluster five-minute discussion that quickly lost steam, getting bogged down in pricing objections due to a complete lack of value being presented.

On Day Nine, you will learn about the three V's of value. For now, just know that not bringing value to your show seldom leads to a sale. Worse than that, it often left the prospect feeling as if they had seen and heard everything they needed from you, making follow-up visits difficult.

In business-to-business sales, follow-up is everything since most sales rarely happen in just one call. That means you need to put on a show more than once, and the quality of that show becomes increasingly important as you get closer to the sale.

It was challenging to show a new rep how the presentation they just bombed could have a different outcome with better samples. Yet it was important to teach them how to create a successful follow-up with even more samples—samples they had previously failed to gather.

When I was a sales rep, I would always ask a prospect to select their favorite sample from among the ones I had shown. I would note the one they chose, then when I returned to my car, I would skim through my remaining samples.

Having plenty of good options enabled me to look for similar ones they might also like. I would review the design elements in those ads and make notes of what the prospect liked and what they didn't. That meant that when I followed up with that prospect, I already had prepared sample ad selections and ideas for them. I could excitedly explain to them how I had kept thinking about their business after our previous meeting and could not wait to share some of the new samples I had found for them.

Without much additional time or effort, I could show a prospect I truly cared about their business—demonstrating I would work hard for them. It showed I was prepared to help them with their advertising needs. Even if a prospect was busy when I approached them for a follow-up, showing them those specifically selected ads and the work I had done on their behalf would, more often than not, persuade them to find time to speak with me. Putting on a good show always helped me move the sale along.

It can be difficult in our fast-paced, crazy lives always to be prepared, hoping someday our chance will come. Everyone wants instant gratification for their efforts. They want to know that the time spent today will pay dividends tomorrow. But as I said on Day One, there are no shortcuts. You must trust that your efforts are worth it. As you go through this book, I hope to show you it will all be worth it, even if sometimes that simply means feeling proud of yourself and the effort you gave. It's important to develop a desire to put on a show because it's the right thing to do and not worry about the outcomes. "Whatever you are, be a good one."

While being prepared is crucial to putting on a show, equally important is being likable. I will continue to remind you I wasn't very good at sales when I started at Clipper, but from Day One, I was extremely likable. (Just ask my mom. I am one of her favorite subjects.)

Not sure how important it is to be likable? It can be everything. Are you likable? Can you get in the habit of being extremely likable? Yes. Yes, you can.

If you already think you are likable, great job! Just finish reading this chapter to see if there are any minor tweaks you want to make. But if you feel this is something you need to work on, pay close attention.

You can create a new brand for yourself based on how likable you are. You just have to understand what it takes: some thought, desire and practice, along with a few new good habits. Start by wanting to be likable.

Perhaps you know someone who prides themselves on not being likable. What are some of their traits? Contrast them with some things you like about people. Think about three or four individuals you trust and respect—mentors, bosses, family, etc. Are any of them likable? How and why?

Let's also build on the gifts you discovered in creating your new car smell during Day Two. That's a promising place to start, but now you need to add in a few often overlooked traits that most of us find likable.

Prepare so every meeting brings your best show.

- Are you typically on time or do you often make people (employers, teammates, friends) wait?
- Do you show up prepared for whatever you're doing?
- Are you coachable or would others describe you as a know-it-all?
- Do you roll up your sleeves and help on projects even when they are not your responsibility?
- Does your body language show care and commitment, even enjoyment, whatever the task?
- Do you engage with people, make eye contact, and show interest or do you check your phone every few minutes?
- Do you turn everything into a conversation about you or do you show interest and ask questions, encouraging others' stories?

When you stop to consider what it means to be likable, are these traits the ones that normally come to mind? It's normal for people to equate being friendly as a key characteristic for being likable, but hopefully this illustrates many of the other factors you can work on too.

Take just a minute to reread the questions above. Then, open your notes and commit to building a habit to improve those traits that will make you more likable. Trust me, we all need to be—and can be—likable.

Being prepared and being likable are two essential elements to "putting on a show," but not the only ones. You also need to be noticed for the right things. Putting on a show aims to help you move ahead and achieve your goals by being noticed and seen in your best light. Whether you're trying to make a sale, improve evaluations at work, earn a sought-after promotion, grow a friendship, or gain the trust needed to manage those reporting to you effectively, the best way to be noticed is to learn what matters to the person you're engaging with.

If you are looking to grow in your current position, discover what aspects of your job your supervisors are most aware of or concerned with. If you are looking to make a sale, discover what features and benefits are most needed by your prospects. Here's the thing, if you know customer service is important to your job, you can't wait until your supervisor is watching and then put on a show. You must make sure that they always see you providing great customer service. Remember, there are no shortcuts.

Let me tell you about John and Mary. I would guess you may have worked with several Johns and as many Marys over the years.

John is the employee who never seems happy in his job. He feels overlooked, overworked, underpaid and mistreated by every supervisor he has ever had. If John's shift begins at 8:00 a.m., he is usually seen parking his car and approaching the time clock anywhere from 7:57 to 8:07 a.m. John may be fun to share a beer with after work, but he is probably not the first person you would hire if you owned the business.

Mary is the opposite. She seems happy to be at work each day. She usually arrives early for her shift. She can even be seen helping customers on her way in, before clocking in for the day. Mary often stays late when the need arises and speaks fondly of her supervisors. When given a new task, even when it is not her responsibility, she is eager to accept.

In the break room, John can be overheard laughing with others at Mary's expense about the effort she makes. "They don't pay me enough to do that," he proudly states. Later, when he hears Mary has received that new promotion, John proclaims, "Naturally, once again, they overlook my time here and give the job to the suck-up."

Whether you like it or not, you are noticed every day. Are you being noticed for the right things? If you don't want to be overlooked, overworked, underpaid or mistreated at work, then put on a show and earn the praise.

Being likable and prepared, and working to be noticed for the right things is a simple but important component of your growth plan; a plan that will enable you to put on your best show every time.

SLOW SPEED BUMP **Spend a few minutes** reflecting on these questions, then add your thoughts to your notes.

- Is your sales presentation stale or are you putting on a show?
- What materials can you add for a stronger presentation?
- How can you improve your emails, messages and virtual presentations?
- Are you able to move sales along that have stalled? What new habit will you use to overcome this?

- What habit will you begin to improve how likable you are?
- Are you doing your best everyday, even when no one is looking? If not, what's stopping you?

Day Five
Business Owners Are from Mars

EVERYONE WORKS FOR SOMEONE, tries to sell to someone, needs to approach someone, or hopes to impress someone. It is important to understand they are all probably from another planet or lost in the Twilight Zone. But what exactly does that mean?

In the last chapter, I discussed how to put on a show—where you work, in everything you do, and with everyone you meet. This plan included being likable, preparedness and being noticed for the right things. It might seem as if that simple plan should be fairly easy to execute, letting you continue on your path to success right now. So what complicates it? Why isn't it that easy?

People!

That's right, people. People will complicate and build obstacles to many of your best intentions. Indeed, many people truly seem to be from another planet (at least on the surface...). You need to work from that realization.

Perhaps you are nodding your head, agreeing with me that business owners are from Mars and communicate differently than those of us from Earth. But that knowledge only helps if you learn how to deal with it properly. Using communication differences as an excuse will not help you grow. Trust me, I have tried to explain to people that they are acting like they are from Mars. Unsurprisingly, they seldom agree.

Many businesses wanted to be part of Clipper Magazine's fall and holiday season mailings since consumers were eager to use the coupons and savings it offered. Their own natural desire to be a part of it made it easy to sell advertising in those mailings. Normally, our holiday magazines were mailed into homes right after Thanksgiving or in early December. We wouldn't publish again until right before Valentine's Day, which was our first book of the new year.

Our books typically needed to be sold out one to two weeks before mailing. That way, we could finalize all the ads, send the book to print, and then mail it out. This would leave us with a slow period from late November until the deadline for that Valentine's Day mailing in mid-January, which would always be much smaller than the holiday issues. Often, it would be the most difficult book of the year to sell ads for, depending on the weather, economy and other factors. Most of our prospecting and sales time for it was in December—which is a busy and stressful time for many business owners. They would routinely tell us, "Yes, I am interested in your winter book, please come and see me in January, when I have time to work on it with you." We would routinely return as requested in early January with our deadline fast approaching, only for them to tell us they had decided to hold off and that we should come back in the spring.

Every year, with client after client, this routine would play out repeatedly. Having experienced it many times as a sales rep, I understood the importance of adjusting my approach in December to have any chance to hit the goals for that Valentine's mailer. When I transitioned into management, I would conduct training sessions for my team every year right after we printed our holiday books. These sessions were entitled, "If a Business Owner Tells Me 'Come and See Me in January,' They Are NOT SOLD!"

You might assume that if a business owner tells you, "I am busy right now, but please come and see me next month for my ad," they will buy ad space. So did I in my first two years as a salesperson. However, by the third year... I should know better, shouldn't I? I needed to understand that business and life are often like the Twilight Zone; things don't always go the way we expect.

The key to my growth then, and yours now, is to understand and even anticipate that things won't go according to plan. I tried for years to teach my sales teams to grasp this, suggesting a few key follow-up techniques in December to help them. While some reps would try these techniques, unfortunately, many others never did. Making excuses for an undersold Valentine's Day mailer was just easier. As you hopefully realized from Day One, it is often far too easy to accept being ground beef than to do the little extras that help you become the Steak. Now that you too understand, the key to your growth will be the steps you take to avoid being sidetracked by miscommunication.

Consider the seasonal changes in your sales cycle. Those selling over a long cycle must always remind themselves, the prospect is *not sold* until they sign. Expect the delays but continually find ways to stay engaged and in their thoughts.

Anticipate that things won't go according to plan.

How can you ensure proper communication? Start by adopting a mindset that can be essential to your success in dealing with people. I have always liked the way author Frederick L. Collins put it:

> Always remember there are two types of people in the world. Those who come into a room and say, "Well, here I am!" and those that say, "Ah, there you are."

The first step is to determine which of these two types you are, and then acknowledge that everyone is hardwired to be one of these two types. Understanding that will help you on the road to increasing empathy and developing the emotional intelligence that will allow you to understand and work with people better.

I was not born as an "Ah, there you are" person; someone who naturally recognized others first. My parental influences and mentors focused more on who I was and how special I was, not on how I should understand and relate to others. So, when I walked into a business, my thoughts went to what I wanted to show them, not necessarily what they wanted to see or were interested in. It took many years of learning (mostly from mistakes) for me to become the type of person I wanted to become.

If, like me, you are more of a "here I am" type person, give some thought to how you could consider the thoughts of others first. I will be covering this in more detail soon, but it's important to understand where you are starting from. Remember how this chapter began: everyone works for someone, tries to sell to someone, needs to approach someone, or hopes to impress someone.

The path to success is understanding that life's encounters aren't about what is in it for you. It's about what is in it for others.

Could it be that without realizing it, others may sometimes sense that *you* are the one from Mars? My wife has said that about me for years. But it wasn't until a few years ago that I finally agreed with her. The sooner you realize that changing your perspective will change how you communicate with others, the closer you will become to continuing your path of growth to success.

This leads to another key component to being other-focused: be a problem solver, not part of the problem. Take a few minutes to think back to a recent issue you encountered.

- What was it and how did it start?
- How was it eventually overcome?
- Were you of assistance?
- What could you have done differently, and how might that have helped?
- Did you participate in finding solutions or did you escalate the problem?
- Did you approach the problem thinking about what was in it for the other person or about how best to help them?

If you looked at my sales at Clipper, you would see that my main problem was that I needed to close more sales. I needed to sell enough ads to publish my magazine and hit my sales quotas to earn the commissions that would support my family. I would often spend several visits and even several hours consulting with a business owner about buying an ad. I would offer insights. I would share proven stories. I would leave them with samples, successful ideas and sometimes even a complete ad campaign design. Equally often, they would decide to hold off. They would choose not to sign with me or even refuse to pay for a completed ad. Trying to explain what was in it for me was seldom a workable solution. I had to find a solution that would be a win for them, which would often result in a win for me as well.

The key was that I needed to want that win for them more than a win for me. That mindset let me do all the little things I might never have done if I was guided more by my own needs and desires. I have worked with many extraordinary sales professionals over the years, but I can probably count on one hand those who achieved success without caring tremendously for their clients' success.

I have discussed how my sales presentations were built on putting on a show and how I would present many sample ads to help create a strong sizzle for that show. Equally important were the fact-finding questions that were a critical part of our discussion. I will cover asking the right questions and properly listening to the answers in a few days, but what you need to understand right now is this: while showing a client the sample ads I could build for them, I needed to uncover answers to three basic questions.

- What do they need?
- What do they want?
- What can they afford?

If I was to be a problem solver and not a part of the problem, I needed to listen for and understand the answers to these three questions.

At Clipper, our most valuable asset was the front cover of our magazine. It was a prestigious spot for a business to place its logo and message. And it had the most visibility of any form of direct mail ad. It was also our most expensive placement. If I spent time showing a small mom-and-pop store owner all our amazing front cover ads and convincing them this was the right product for them, I might well be creating a problem for them. Most would absolutely want that kind of exposure. They might even be able to afford it. But if it weren't what they truly needed and if their return from that ad didn't cover the expenses, that would be a problem for them—and for me, since this would probably be the last time they ran an ad with me. Just ask yourself, before looking for your own win, "What's in it for them?"

Reflect on the type of person you want to be. There are no shortcuts, so you will have to challenge yourself. Today and each day, challenge yourself to make no excuses and to be a problem solver. Ask yourself, "What is in it for them?" Then you will run into fewer Martians and find your encounters resulting in wins for everyone.

SLOW SPEED BUMP | **Spend a few minutes** reflecting on these questions, then add your thoughts to your notes.

- Who are you most trying to impress? How do you communicate with them? What can you do to improve your communication?

- What excuse have you used for not accomplishing things in your career? What new perspective might you consider now?

- If you are not an "Ah, there you are" type person, would you like to be? What can you do to develop that way?

- Does your presentation uncover what a prospect needs, wants and can afford? If not, consider probing questions and techniques to better discover those.

- What appointments, calls or virtual meetings do you have today? Ask yourself first, "What's in it for them?"

Do nothing out of selfish ambition or vain conceit. Rather, in humility value others above yourselves.

Philippians 2:3

Day Six
Words Have Meaning

ONE OF THE MOST ICONIC TV COMMERCIALS of my lifetime first aired in January 1984.

```
        Three elderly ladies are examining a
massive hamburger at "Home of the Big Bun."
Lady 1:    It certainly is a big bun.
Lady 2:    It's a very big bun.
Lady 1:    A big fluffy bun.
Lady 2:    It's a very big fluffy bun.
Lady 3:    Where's the beef?
Narrator:  You want something better.
           You're Wendy's kind of people.
```

The message in Wendy's "Where's the Beef" spot was clear. Wendy's hamburgers had more beef than their competitors. Simply stated. Visually supported. Fun to say and easy to remember.

Now, tell me about yourself and the brand you represent. That is, open your notes and write a thirty-second commercial about the value you hope to bring to each prospect. Write it as if you are speaking directly to the person.

- Who are you?
- Why are you here today?
- What are you hoping to discuss with me?
- What are you selling?
- What is so great about your product or service that you have decided to speak to me about it?

Great! You just finished writing an amazing thirty-second spot about how your product can help someone, right? Was it simply stated and can it be visually supported? Come on, this should be the easiest assignment I give out in these twenty-one days. After all, you spend quite a bit of time with yourself. If you are in sales, you must spend many hours a week speaking with people. Remember, these thirty seconds are a foundational part of those crucial first sixty seconds in every encounter you have, so it's important to be clear while you succinctly introduce yourself and your offer.

So many hours are spent speaking every day, for so long, that most people never stop to listen to those words or consider their meaning or their impact on others.

"Where's the beef?" Three little words that convey so much meaning.

Today, you will develop a strong thirty-second commercial to introduce yourself and your brand. This simple exercise can bolster your inner confidence. In fact, it's possibly the most crucial building block for your personal confidence.

Have you ever been at a networking event where you interacted with many people you didn't know? Have you avoided joining or initiating conversations because of a lack of confidence? If you have ever wondered what to say or worried about what someone may think or ask, this changes as of today.

Take the time to draft a commercial for you and your product. This is your "value statement." Have fun with it! The key is for it to be passionate, easy-to-say and memorable for the person hearing it. Don't worry about whether it is perfect; just get it started. It will undoubtedly change over the next several days. (Trust me.) You may even develop a few commercial "spots" to share in different situations. Having this commercial planned out in advance will make it easier to introduce yourself, even when you don't know the people you're with and you're not feeling especially confident.

The key to a successful spot, along with being fun, passionate, etc., is how you deliver it. You and I may share the same value statement. But whoever can deliver it with confidence, strong eye contact, positive body language, and pride will deliver it best.

Remember your gifts? Make sure you use them here. They will help forge the confidence and ease you need. If you have a few minutes, I invite you to record your thirty-second commercial and send it to me at emeraldlakebooks.com/bloomer. I'd love to hear what you develop and provide a little feedback if you're interested.

For many years, as a sales manager with Clipper, my favorite role was that of a coach, which often involved going along on a full-day ride with a sales rep. I would leave my home early each morning and travel throughout the state to meet with the rep I

Deliver your value statement with confidence and pride.

was helping that day. This was particularly enjoyable in a state like New Jersey, which should be known for its amazing local diners. We would arrive at a diner and, over coffee and breakfast, discuss the upcoming day. The rep knew well in advance I was coming and was often very prepared, with a full slate of appointments.

Despite that planning, most appointments would unfortunately begin the same way. As the business owner or decision maker approached us and asked their first question (often "why are you here?"), the sales rep wouldn't answer but instead slowly turned and looked in my direction. Imagine how much better it would have been if they had a strong, confident, well-rehearsed value statement. You will know your value statement is ready when you can deliver it confidently every time—even when your supervisor is standing next to you.

Now that you have started working on your value statement, it's important to address the infinite ways words have meaning—words that will be a key component in helping you:

- build rapport
- gain trust and respect
- communicate professionally

Businessman and author Stephen Covey said:

> Most people do not listen with the intent to understand; they listen with the intent to reply. They're either speaking or preparing to speak. They're filtering everything through their own paradigms, reading their autobiography into other people's lives.

While it has taken me years to understand this quote fully, I have seen countless examples of it in action. Building rapport.

Gaining trust and respect. Communicating professionally. These only happen when you stop filtering words through your own perspective. For your words to have the meaning you hope for, you must truly *listen* to others, and not first with the intent to reply. Active listening means paying attention to what's being said, even if you must wait to formulate a response. I witnessed this almost daily in my years as a sales manager, but it still took years to understand.

Those ride-along days were highly effective for coaching and teaching my sales reps. Their main goal, however, was to generate sales. Most reps I rode with would try to fill our day with as many prospects as possible who were close to buying. They had already seen that many of these appointments would result in sales when we rode together. This had helped me earn a reputation as a strong closer and a valuable asset to their day. Many of my reps would eagerly look forward to our days together.

While I would love to tell you I was an awesome closer, it takes delving deeper into the Stephen Covey quote to see what was actually happening here. Often, when a salesperson is speaking to a prospect, they are so focused on having a proper *reply* ready, that they fail to *listen* to what the prospect is saying.

As an interested bystander, I had the opportunity to listen, read their body language, and observe little behaviors that showed interest (or lack thereof). I could get a sense of what the prospect might need to be shown or what their real questions or concerns were. I was in a position to direct the conversation where it needed to go based on the prospect's frame of reference, not the rep's.

I learned the key was truly *listening* before replying. Words have meaning when you speak them, but they often have the desired results only when they are addressing the prospect's concerns.

Have you ever lain awake at night replaying a conversation you had with someone hours before? That's because your mind is still processing the conversation with an intent to understand. Unfortunately, a need to reply often makes people act too quickly. It is only much later when you start to rethink and realize that what you replied to wasn't exactly what they said or how you should have replied. After that, it's common to question your actual reply, afraid you missed something.

What can you learn from this, and what good habit can you pick up today? Slow down and try to listen completely to a person before framing your answer. It is better to have a brief thoughtful pause followed by a correct response with what you really wanted to say than a quick reply that misses the true point. In effect, try to be an interested bystander to the conversation, not just provide a quick response.

I mentioned earlier that one of my gifts was humor. I have often made a brief humorous comment or asked a question to give myself time to think... and then, here we go!

You need to hear words and use them confidently, for they are important to your success. You also need to always keep in mind their impact on others.

Author Rachel Wolchin reminds us:

> Be mindful when it comes to your words. A string of some that don't mean much to you, may stick with someone else for a lifetime.

Are you still working on your value statement? Remember when I told you it would probably change several times over the next few days? Well, reread yours now. I asked you to cover:

- Who are you?
- Why are you here today?
- What are you hoping to discuss with me?
- What are you selling?
- What is so great about your product or service that you have decided to speak to me about it?

Let me ask you, from whose perspective did you write about the value? You take your value statement to the next level when you deliver it to the frame of reference of the person you are speaking to. Here is who I am and why I am here, and why I feel it may interest you. I feel this is great about my product or service, and this is how it can benefit you. It is more about them, their needs, and how your product can help, than about you and what you have to offer.

Have you written from this viewpoint? If not, no worries, you will get there. For now, simply start thinking about your words more carefully than you ever have before. Trust me, you will be glad you did.

SLOW SPEED BUMP

Spend a few minutes reflecting on these questions, then add your thoughts to your notes.

- Have you developed a strong initial value statement? Here is an example as a reference.

> "Hi. I'm Tom of Bloomer Associates. I would love to show you how we've been helping other organizations assess, hire and train their sales teams. Our goal is to engage and inspire your team while allowing you the freedom to focus on your products and customers. Many of our current clients are struggling with training new sellers while motivating veteran reps to reach difficult quotas. I'll be glad to show how we build a coaching approach that will meet your unique needs. We have spent over thirty years in the field as proven sales leaders and bring a hands-on practical expertise most trainers can't offer."

- If you haven't developed a value statement yet, how will you develop it?
- Think about ways you can give yourself time to slow down and listen. How will you begin a new habit of making a conscious effort to slow down and listen?
- What questions or materials can you routinely have at the ready?

Day Seven
Even When No One is Watching

BASEBALL IS A REMARKABLY SIMPLE GAME. A pitcher pitches a ball. A batter swings his bat, trying to make contact with the ball. When he makes contact, it can sometimes result in a base hit. Each batter's results are measured by how many hits they get. A Major League batter that averages three hits out of every ten at-bats may be headed to the Hall of Fame. They will absolutely be considered an all-star. But a batter that only averages two hits out of every ten at-bats will most likely find themselves looking for a new career—unless, of course, they can throw a baseball over 90 mph for strikes.

The margin for error is exceptionally small—both in baseball and in most career achievements. The question to answer is, "What does it take to accomplish great results?" What does it take to get that one more hit out of every ten tries? What does it take for an average salesperson to close one more sale every week? What does it take to add one more quality prospect every day?

As a boy, I dreamed of being a professional baseball player. I would beg my younger brother to play catch practically every summer day. I angered my mom when she discovered the dented aluminum siding on our home—dents that were formed when I attempted to play even when my brother chose not to. I still remember waiting patiently for my father to return from work in the evenings. Ball and glove in hand, I waited in the front yard. I would play baseball from age five through my sophomore year of high school.

Sadly, however, a professional baseball career wasn't in the cards for me. One of my earliest lessons in rejection came as a sophomore on junior varsity cut day, the day when we learned who made the team and who did not. I still wonder whether my demise was my inability to hit a curve ball or my lack of stature. I was barely 5′ tall throughout most of high school and a paltry one hundred pounds—after dinner. Whatever the reason, I needed to look for a new career.

I can still remember all those days when my dad would arrive home from work. At that age, I could not understand how tired he must have been. You see, my dad worked at a Pennsylvania stone quarry and typically left for the forty-minute commute to work by 5:30 a.m. He would arrive home after 5:00 p.m. and would also work half days most Saturdays. What he learned to expect was that when he arrived home, I would be waiting to play catch and we would play each time right until dinner was ready.

I told you on Day One I believe it was my desire to work harder than practically anyone I ever met that made me successful. We can debate whether we are born with our work ethic or develop it, but I believe mine came from watching my father and others live out a work ethic that I would later emulate.

You are responsible for who you become and for how you handle what life brings us. The effort you put into all aspects of your life is up to you. Some may argue that others are born with a silver spoon or they're born with all the talent. You may say, "It's not what you know. It's who you know." I can't tell you these things don't matter. Of course they do! But what I want you to realize is that these things are simply one part of the equation. It comes down to using the gifts you have been given and making the most of them. Your attitude, desire and work ethic are much more important than anything else.

How does this help you today? We can all probably agree that work ethic matters, or at least helps. Knowing I need to hit a curve ball is important, but I still have to work hard to pull it off.

This chapter is all about finding the daily motivation crucial to nurturing a strong work ethic. You must want it even when no one else is watching. You must want to stay out in the field looking for that one more strong prospect, even when your supervisor just criticized your results. You must have a confident, energized presentation in a big sales call, even when you spent the morning arguing with your spouse or best friend.

This want came easily for me in the early years of building my career. It was far more difficult later, after the small entrepreneurial company I joined in 1992 was sold a few times in the 2000s (and a new corporate culture was established). When I worked for a small business founder that motivated and inspired, having a strong work ethic was easy. Twenty-five years later, working for a large holding company that barely knew my name was far more challenging. As I got closer to the day when they would eliminate my position—one I had spent most of my adult life developing into a job I loved—it became increasingly difficult

You earn success when no one is watching.

to stay motivated. I often had to ask myself, "Why? Who am I working for at this point?"

We all need to do our best. Not for the supervisor who criticizes us, not for the company that doesn't care about or know us, not for Facebook or our neighbor. Personally, I strive to do my best because I believe this is what God wants: to be my best at anything I do. But when my job was coming to an end, I needed to be reminded why my dad always found that extra time for me, why I worked the way I did back in the day, why I still needed and wanted to work the same way. I believe God is watching, and I want to be the best he wants me to be. This makes me happy and keeps me energized.

You need to find your own motivation for being the best you can be. This protects you against the boss, the spouse, the parent, the friend, or any other influence in your life that can sap the work ethic you need. Many of us can relate to the obstacles people erect against our growth and success. The key lies in not only seeing them but finding the inner resolve to move beyond them.

On Day Four, I mentioned my two kids. I'd like to tell you more about my son, Ryan. He eventually grew up and outgrew his car seat. He moved out of our family home and one day, in his twenties, he went to work for a restaurant chain—a midsize chain based in the southern US preparing to open its first locations in New Jersey. They were looking for managers, and with Ryan's background in food service, he seemed like a perfect fit. He would work for this chain twice over his career. Both times, he was led along a similar track.

The first time, newly hired for their southern New Jersey opening, he left for a six-week training program in Florida. He loved it. His training manager gave him a glowing endorsement. Ryan even considered moving to Florida for an opening they expected soon. He thrived in their atmosphere. The store was fast-paced, the leadership was helpful, and the team was part of an amazing culture. He gained confidence in applying his strong customer service skills and his ability to work hard and be a team player. His six weeks flew by, and he barely missed home. His training taught him all he needed to get started with the grand opening in New Jersey. He flew home excited to begin.

That all ended within a week, immediately upon his return. He encountered a completely different management approach than the team he had trained with, which was significantly less supportive. This new approach shattered his confidence. The culture and support he had seen in Florida were nowhere to be found in the restaurant that would be his daily workplace. The well-oiled team he had trained with was replaced with a struggling, disinterested group of trainees. The leadership was critical and unhelpful—this after he had worked side-by-side with leaders who rolled up their sleeves and pitched in to help during busy times. Young Ryan wanted no part of this. One week convinced him that the food industry wasn't where he belonged or wanted to be.

Fast forward a few years later, and Ryan, now in his late twenties, was still searching for a career that felt right. He relocated to Fayetteville, North Carolina, near his sister Kayla, who had traveled there a few years earlier for her own career. Ryan loved North Carolina but wasn't happy with his current job. He had a text conversation with the manager who trained him in Florida, the one who gave him a strong recommendation and whom he enjoyed working with. That manager had become a recruiter for the same chain, covering the southeast, and they needed a manager in Cary, North Carolina, a town about ninety minutes away from where Ryan was living. After much consideration, he decided to take a second chance with this chain. The North Carolina franchise group seemed different from the New Jersey group—and hopefully more like Florida.

He again had an amazing experience while training, this time at the store close to home in Fayetteville. He spent six weeks training, as well as finding a new apartment in Cary, close to his new store. After moving in and starting work, he slowly began to see differences in the management and culture. Unlike the New Jersey experience, the issues here were much subtler: a disinterested store manager, a constantly understaffed team, a somewhat abusive and uninspiring corporate training leader. Late-twenties Ryan had matured since his New Jersey days. Despite his concerns, he tried to work his way through it and create the culture he was looking for. As a result, he stayed with the chain for close to a year before finding another opportunity to begin again.

My son had to learn the hard way that we must often deal with difficult people. In our careers, there will almost always be obstacles, including the manager who doesn't care or is a poor leader, and the team that can simply drain your desire to work over eight hours. I am sure many would have decided it wasn't worth it. Are you experiencing these feelings, but seem trapped in a situation you can't afford to leave?

As Ryan continued on and grew into a strong manager, he learned that his efforts were for his own sense of pride, even when no one else was watching. As he continues in his career, he now hopes to be a positive influence on others, especially those reporting to him, looking for a culture they want to be a part of.

The habit I hope you develop today is to find the desire to manage yourself through the noise, discouragement and difficult times. Do not let others destroy your day, your job, your experience, your opportunity, or your chance for success. Find the inner resolve to work through challenges for yourself. It doesn't matter who is watching or managing you. From today on, have the desire to manage yourself.

SLOW SPEED BUMP

Spend a few minutes reflecting on these questions, then add your thoughts to your notes.

- Are you experiencing noise, discouragement or tough times in your career right now? If so, describe the issue you're facing.

- What will you do to manage through it?

- Has someone's influence prevented you from growing to where you hope to be? What steps will you take to break that influence?

- What are some things you should do each day, even though no one is watching? Things you know will help your sales?

Whatever you do, work at it with all your heart, as working for the Lord, not for human masters, since you know that you will receive an inheritance from the Lord as a reward. It is the Lord Christ you are serving.

Colossians 3:23–24

Day Eight
Dunkin' Versus Starbucks

HAVE YOU EVER HEARD THE PHRASE, "Let's get ready to rumble?" When you hear it, you may anticipate that something exciting is about to happen. This iconic catchphrase, coined by Michael Buffer, gained enormous popularity around 1984 and has been used to open many an event since then. None however is as compelling as today's discussion: the battle between Dunkin' and Starbucks for our coffee preferences.

I must admit I have been a Dunkin' fan since way back. Come on, coffee and doughnuts? I challenge you to show me a better way to start my day. Need a sausage croissant? They've got you covered. Prefer your coffee iced or, my wife's obsession, pumpkin flavored? They've got you covered. As you have gotten to know me, you've probably figured out that the blue-collar hometown feel of their messaging resonated with me. "It's time to make the doughnuts." Heck, yeah! Get up early and make those fresh doughnuts, I am on my way! If they tell me "America runs on Dunkin'," I am all in.

Do you know the slogan for Starbucks? Me neither, I had to look it up. Do you find them overpriced? Me too. And seriously, what is a Venti? On the rare occasions when I had no choice but to order at Starbucks, I felt out of place. Like I didn't belong, and everyone working there and in line knew it.

This angst would become one of my favorite training class ice breakers (along with a debate on morning people versus night owls, but I digress). During our weeklong corporate sales training sessions, I found Tuesday mornings were often the most difficult for attendees. Many had long flights or drives on Monday, followed by a late afternoon session. Starting at 8:00 a.m. on Tuesday morning in Lancaster, Pennsylvania, could be a rude awakening (especially for our West Coast attendees). So, I would begin with the debate on Dunkin' versus Starbucks. I joyfully explained why Dunkin' folks were simply nicer people—more awake and more receptive than the others. Starbucks folks typically seemed very elitist and standoffish. It was a fun way to get the group moving and contributing and would help launch us into a conversation on reading our customers.

At this point, I have either offended you and left you wondering where this chapter is headed. Flash forward to 2019. My wife and I had just moved from New Jersey to Apex, North Carolina. We were in a new home, meeting new people and trying to establish our new routine. For me, that meant finding the closest Dunkin'. News flash! Unlike New Jersey, there isn't a Dunkin' on every corner in North Carolina. I couldn't take my morning walk and stop in for my coffee and a doughnut.

I did find a Dunkin' only ten minutes away, though. No worries, right? Well, I soon learned the employees there move quite a bit slower. They are also not staffed the same, and they don't know my name. They seem to have trouble even making my coffee correctly. How difficult could cream and sugar be?

As you may have guessed, stubborn man that I am, I kept going. My wife would shake her head and smile every time I arrived home unhappy. Remember, my chief pleasure was the enjoyment and relaxation that my morning coffee used to bring me.

Once as I was beginning my Clipper workday, Chris Gimber, our sales division Human Resources professional, and I were speaking over Zoom. While she was enjoying her Starbucks coffee, I decided to see where the closest Starbucks was. It was within walking distance! But I couldn't, could I? Maybe it would be better than continuing to suffer with my Dunkin' dilemma.

Well, I am now a believer in Starbucks coffee. I know the Venti is the large size I am looking for. I proudly pay and claim rewards with my Starbucks phone app. I discovered that Starbucks employees are just as nice as my former Dunkin' friends. I now have an enjoyable and relaxing conversation every morning with Lanette as she makes my coffee. I don't even enjoy iced Dunkin' coffee anymore, as I have gotten used to the flavor of Starbucks. Who saw that coming? Certainly not me! But after a long struggle, I was finally open to change, and I am now much happier for it.

Before moving on, since you listened to my coffee story, I would love to hear yours. Connect with me on LinkedIn and message me your preference for either Dunkin' or Starbucks. I look forward to our discussion or further debate.

There is a famous line from Bruce, the shark in Disney's animated film, *Finding Nemo*.

> If I am to change this image, I must first change myself. Fish are friends, not food.

While there are many quotes about change and change management, this has always been one of my favorites. Can you think of a more difficult change to make? Can you imagine any creature less self-aware than a shark? Wouldn't it be infinitely more challenging for Bruce to give up fish for food than for me to switch favorite coffees?

I like to think of this quote when I am confronted with change. As author and educator Karen Kaiser Clark said:

> Life is change. Growth is optional. Choose wisely.

If there is one important lesson I have learned in my career and life, it is this. Change will happen. Change must happen. Growth, however, is optional.

There are countless stories I could share regarding change. Yet one stands out in particular for me. I went through a major career change back before my time with Clipper. While working in postsecondary education, the company I was with started its own advertising division. I had no knowledge of or interest in sales, but I found myself thrust into a life full of daily rejection. I went from a comfortable office setting to days out on the street selling (or trying to) door-to-door. I can tell you today this career move was absolutely the best I could have made. A year later, I started working for Clipper, with the adjustments that went along with that. Again, absolutely the best change I could have made.

Some changes are thrust upon you, but there are also those you discover and contemplate on your own. For many, it seems the changes you didn't choose are the most difficult to adapt to.

I think it's clear how much I enjoyed my time with Clipper. It was a great opportunity for me. I worked with so many amazing people over the years and built many strong friendships. I have been able to provide for my family and grow as a leader. Life is change. The company I loved and worked for over the course of more than twenty-eight years went through many cultural shifts. Every time a major reorganization happened at Clipper, I saw some people prosper and others falter. Some talented people left after one upheaval or another. Some sales reps struggled to perform when they had to adapt to the many changes to our business model. For years, we heard, "Print is dying. Print is dead." We had to adapt to stay relevant to our advertisers. Had I given up when we were first warned that print was dying, I would have missed out on my most successful years with Clipper.

In the summer of 2003, in a dark and dismal conference room in Lancaster, Pennsylvania, in an otherwise gorgeous luxury hotel, one of my biggest career changes was thrust upon me. Our Clipper leadership team held periodic all-day conferences in this basement room, and most were enjoyable, informative and collaborative. This particular morning, however, we learned that the founders of Clipper would announce later in the day that they had been acquired by Gannett. A core group of about a dozen leaders sat stunned and silent. This group had lived and breathed Clipper as a daily passion for a decade or more. The dreams of conquering the world of direct mail and retiring

Learn to trust and welcome change.

early after helping take our company nationwide were quickly replaced with fears of job hunting on the near horizon. For Kelly and me, it was a nerve-wracking time. We had just taken a huge risk and bought a vacation home the month prior. Our family budget was stretched further than ever before.

The sixteen years after the sale of Clipper would become the best of my career. They would be different and more difficult. Each day, I lived with a constant fear for tomorrow. But growth was an option, and I took it. Unfortunately, some great people did not. The culture had changed. The company no longer had a small family atmosphere, but this wasn't necessarily a bad thing. Luckily for us, the founders stayed on at Clipper for another ten years. Their eventual departure would bring about another change—another door. A few years after they left, Clipper would be acquired again by another company that ultimately eliminated my position. But even that was five years later than many had predicted.

Spending time discovering key behaviors and habits to form the foundation for your success will be meaningless if you can't adapt to change, learning how to trust and welcome it. I hope you spend a few minutes opening yourself to some of the changes in habits I have already covered. But if nothing else, please open yourself to changes that will come your way moving forward. For me, change—often unwanted—has led to some of life's greatest gifts.

SLOW SPEED BUMP

Spend a few minutes reflecting on these questions, then add your thoughts to your notes.

- Is there a change you know you should make but have been avoiding? If so, what is it? Why do you think you've been avoiding it?

- How might making a few changes to your sales process or presentation increase your sales if you implemented them? Consider changes you've avoided but that are helping your peers and competition.

"Have I not commanded you? Be strong and courageous. Do not be afraid; do not be discouraged, for the Lord your God will be with you wherever you go."

Joshua 1:9

Day Nine
The Three *V*'s of Value

The LATE 1990S WAS A FANTASTIC TIME to be in advertising sales. Not only was Clipper expanding at an amazing pace and growing nationally, so too were many of our competitors. The variety of ways for small business owners to market themselves was constantly expanding.

Late in the summer of 1999, our company founders asked me to tour our regions throughout the country to re-train our sales teams. The issue was the decreasing rate these markets were receiving for their ads. While I addressed proper ways to prospect, overcome objections, and use negotiation techniques, my primary goal was to help our teams realize and communicate their value better.

Here's an excerpt from one of my sales seminars.

> The reality of our world is that we need our business customers more than they need us. Let's face the facts. There are many ways that a business can advertise in today's world. For each Clipper Magazine area that we sell, there are dozens of sales reps for other companies competing for that same ad dollar. It is just not fair... It is war!

> Why is it that some Clipper Magazines average over forty pages per issue, while others struggle for twenty-four pages of good offers? Why is it that some new areas barely premiere at sixteen pages with low rates? And others open at thirty-two pages for good money and with the best names in town? Simply put, some Clipper reps realize that in an advertising war, Clipper outfits its reps with machine guns and aerial support, while most of the competition is just throwing stones. So why then, if our reps are holding machine guns, do they only fight back with stones themselves?

We understood that in the direct mail world, Clipper had as strong a value proposition as anyone else. We delivered a high-quality advertising program that got results at an affordable price. In many markets, our magazines were the best place for local small and medium-sized businesses to place their trust and ad dollars. So what was the problem?

Too many sales reps struggled with ways to demonstrate that value. Hours and days of repeated rejection reduced many reps to desperation... and their belief in the value quickly disappeared. Far too often, they would take the sale, any sale, even when they were only able to get the same price that far less valuable direct mail ads were charging.

Anyone who has successfully spent time in sales understands how crucial value is. That's one reason I had you spend so much time earlier working on your thirty-second value statement. (Does yours include machine gun fire or are you simply throwing stones?)

Motivational speaker Jim Rohn said:

> You don't get paid for the hour. You get paid for the value you bring to the hour.

Let that sink in. Trust me when I tell you I have coached many salespeople who were more than willing to put in the extra hours. They failed, however, to bring any added value to those hours.

Many sales reps fail to grasp the difference. Too many of our sales teams were struggling to champion Clipper's value. They felt as though showing up with a quality product and representing a great organization should be enough. They wanted simply to be paid for their hour. They failed to see they were getting paid for the actual value they brought to each potential sale.

I was fortunate in my early sales career not to be good at sales. It led me to do all those little extra things, and to understand and eventually master what I like to call "the three V's of value."

- Be value: Why are you here today?
- Bring value: What are you bringing in to show this prospect?
- Offer value: How do you hope to be of benefit to them?

I would sometimes travel up to two hours, fighting traffic to arrive at an early morning meeting with a sales rep. We would discuss our appointments for the day, travel to our first one... and then it would happen. Time and again, as I stepped out of the passenger side of the car, I noticed the sales rep exiting the car empty-handed—without having spent even a few minutes assembling the presentation tools needed for the call.

Be value. Bring value. Offer value.

I would naively ask, "What do you need to bring in for today's appointment?"

They would reply, "All good. I showed them everything before. I don't need anything new today."

I'll ask you what I always asked them.

- Why are you here today?
- If you showed them everything before, why didn't they buy then?
- Don't you have a benefit to share with them today?

Like many, you may feel you have it all covered, but I would implore you to ask yourself if you really have all the tools you need. Will you be showing value by throwing stones or will you be impressing your prospect with machine guns and aerial support?

Why was I so confident in sharing value with my ad samples? I unquestionably had the best-looking direct mail magazine in the market. When I spoke with a prospect or client, I always had several magazine ads open in front of us. This would reinforce the beauty of our designs and quality of our ads throughout my presentation. I would bring strong testimonials and share stories of past successful campaigns. Strong storytelling accompanied by testimonials and referrals is a proven winner in sales. Of course, they take some time to gather, learn and use. But I understood I got paid for the value I brought to the hour.

Whatever you are selling or whoever you are meeting with, always ask yourself, "Am I bringing all three *V*'s of value to the relationship I'm trying to build today?"

When you genuinely believe in the value you offer, your natural gifts and your confidence will increase. Spend time learning from successful people where you work or live. I asked you on Day Four to think about three or four people you trusted and respected. I guarantee you those people bring value to you.

In the summer of 1999, while many reps were struggling with bringing value to their prospects and clients, a favorite peer of mine was not. One of our most successful regions was Albany, New York. Years later, the Clipper market created there by David Marks still reigns as one of the finest. David just plain got it. He not only understood how to provide value, but found creative ways to have his favorite employee show it for him. This employee would build value every month for over 80,000 homes, over 200,000 readers, and the many small and medium-sized businesses in town. You see, David understood value. He brought creativity to a new level at Clipper.

So, who was his favorite employee? It was his Albany Clipper Magazine. David understood his magazine could offer value every day to consumers, as well as business owners. He could create a product that would be of value with every mailing.

David coined the Clipper phrase "Open. Read. Keep." He knew that the front cover ad needed to compel you to open the book. He understood that the next few pages needed to be the most valuable offers from the most desirable businesses, which would keep the book in your home. Open. Read. Keep.

To this day, the book David built brings value to consumers, and thus to the business owners advertising their services inside. Is his book simply throwing stones? I think not.

I hope you will spend time today updating your notes and pondering all the ways you can use the three *V*'s of value, and that you look for ways to use your unique gifts creatively, as David did. Want to present the best value you can to your prospects and clients? Use your best assets. Spend time with successful people. Ask your customers what value they see in your product or service. Why do they work with you? Be confident and bring value. The more value you bring, the more confident you will be.

A few brief thoughts on follow-up... Remember the simple questions I asked while exiting the car on those ride-alongs? Why are you here, and so on?

I have learned over the years that little happens at first sight, except maybe love. I should share how I first met my wife, but truth be told, it was only love at first sight for me. But I digress. I wanted to mention the importance of follow-ups.

It is important in all you do, both in sales and in life, that you bring value by how you follow through with things. Most sales happen days, sometimes weeks, after the initial presentation. Strong friendships happen as a relationship grows over time. Bringing value in how you follow through in life can make a huge difference. Remembering names and important events, thoughtful notes of encouragement at the right times, sharing news or posts you see that you know someone may be interested in, showing just the right sample on just the right day...

The three *V*'s of value need to be part of every relationship you hope to build.

SLOW SPEED BUMP

Spend a few minutes reflecting on these questions, then add your thoughts to your notes.

- How can you be of more value to your clients?
- What creative ways can you use to show more value to your prospects?
- What materials or other ideas can you add to your presentations to provide more value?
- Is there a bonus you can offer prospects who take action? How about an incentive for some of your lost or stalled prospects?

Day Ten
Play Hard, Work Hard

IF ONLY THE IMPORTANT LIFE LESSONS for me could have happened as Paul Simon spoke in his 1973 hit, "Kodachrome," where he discusses all the things he didn't learn in high school. And how, his lack of education didn't hurt him, even though he could read the writing on the wall.

For today's chapter, I will try to make an important concept as obvious as it was for Paul Simon. To be successful, you must find a strong work/life balance. True success can only exist when you are also happy and fulfilled. The only real question then is which comes first. Must you work exceedingly hard in the hope of someday being able to play and enjoy life? Or must you first play hard and use that excitement and enjoyment to drive you toward success?

When I was growing up, my baby boomer generation was expected to work hard first. Indeed, enjoyment wasn't even guaranteed. Work hard and then see what happens. That is what I was always taught to believe.

What I have found over the years is that life doesn't always follow that script. In fact, I would now argue that some of my biggest successes, some of the times I was working the hardest, came about because of a sense that I was actually at play. Playing hard often inspires, refreshes and strengthens us—leading to better and more productive work. Many of today's top employers have discovered this. Sadly, others have not.

I said on Day One that my goal was to push you, to ask you to work harder for yourself than you ever have before. You must stretch yourself. I have witnessed so many people stretch themselves over the years and seen them grow and achieve as a result. I have also seen others not want to commit to stretching themselves, or who simply stretched too hard and broke. I have rarely seen anyone stretch themselves more than my daughter, Kayla, though.

Even as a child, our daughter pushed herself harder than we ever could. She had a fierce desire to be the best at everything she tried. I would marvel at the mere sight of her on the monkey bars at the neighborhood park. She wouldn't give up, she would will herself to pull hand over hand, swaying and holding her body above the ground until she reached the other side. If she fell, she got up, went back to the beginning, and started again. Sporting activities, class work, football with her older brother... her desire to be the best never wavered. As she continued through high school and into college, I watched as she studied for hours and committed herself to every course, every paper, every grade.

For Kayla, each effort had to be her best. She wanted to excel at everything she tried. She worked her way through college, then spent two years working and interning in her field while attending evening classes for her master's degree. Pushing yourself that hard for that long can be taxing on your emotions.

Thankfully, Kayla always had an incredible appetite for play as well. She played just as hard as she worked. Many of the activities at which she worked so hard were true passions and brought her immense pride and satisfaction. She began riding horses when she was six and still rides to this day. She has worked herself hard for competitions and in practice, but if you asked her, she would never call it work. Playing hard and working hard seem to happen together for her, not one before or because of the other.

I still remember an emotional drive we had as she was about to complete her master's degree. She had moved back home for two years after living away for her first four years of college. After those two long and stressful years, she was eager to receive her accreditations and just as eager to become more independent. She informed me she was hoping to move away from home. She had found a recruiter and, within a few short months, would move nine hours from home to Fayetteville, North Carolina, where she would start her new career in a new home, completely on her own. She would have no choice but to work hard. She would also continue to play hard.

I have heard many people speak about stretching themselves, and about pushing themselves to excel and setting a goal to be their best. Our church pastor once spoke about this during his sermon in a way that really hit home for me. He talked about the need to stretch ourselves to grow. When you exercise, you stretch your muscles; this constant stretching and relaxing enables a muscle to grow. Whether you're growing your faith or your ability for success, that growth can only come after you stretch beyond your starting point.

If you hope to manage yourself to success, you must first be willing to stretch yourself. Do things you have been afraid to do. At times, stretching yourself will make you happier than ever before.

Take a moment to look around at the people in your life—family, friends, co-workers. Do they seem to have a good work/life balance?

Too often, I instead find signs of people:

- not wanting to be accountable
- not taking responsibility
- not being persistent

Roger Staubach once said:

There are no traffic jams along the extra mile.

The extra mile is where you find those people who stretch themselves.

There is a reason Roger was one of my childhood heroes. In character, work effort and teamwork, he represented so much of what I valued in life—from his days in the Navy, serving our country, to his actions on the football field, and in his community after he retired from the game.

Write these four things in your notes today:

- I will be accountable for my success and happiness.
- I am the only one responsible for my success and happiness.
- I will be persistent in my efforts toward success and happiness.
- I will be found on that extra mile leading to my success and happiness.

Managing yourself to success was never going to be easy. But those four commitments are actually the hardest part. They're where you begin your path to that extra mile.

When you stop passing the buck, which is far too easy to do, you begin to stretch. When you are stretching to accomplish new things, they often transition from hard work to hard play. Hard play motivates you to play harder, and then you work harder and enjoy more success.

Either way, the key is to find the proper work/life balance. You can't continuously stretch yourself. You need opportunities to enjoy rewards and play along the way. Incorporating more play into your workday creates a more satisfying experience. Often when work is simply work, finding balance is all about getting proper rest and finding and enjoying little rewards along the way. Watching my daughter work through stressful times has given me a greater appreciation of how to accomplish work/life balance. It's important to find your play in life and to seek meaningful rewards to feel a proper balance. You cannot simply stretch all the time.

Two stories from my Clipper days may help illustrate my path...

There was a time in my early years at Clipper when I never considered a single hour of what I did to be work. During my second year there, I received a new supervisor. Rob Liss had recently joined the company, and though he eventually relocated to Lancaster near our corporate office, when he started, he was still living on Long Island in New York. Rob was hired to become Clipper's Executive VP of Sales and oversee our growth. His first regions, besides my New Jersey markets, were

Do the things you have been afraid to do.

Maryland and eventually Virginia. Rob cut his teeth by riding along with and managing Clipper sales reps in those three states. Despite a three-hour commute, my territory was still the closest to his home. Rob would schedule a ride with me about every three weeks. I put a lot of planning and thought into those days, making sure to have plenty of promising appointments and a packed day. I had to make sure I would impress my supervisor.

Unfortunately for Rob, many of his reps would cancel their day with him early the same morning or late the night before. Since I was so close by, I routinely got the call, "Hey, Tom. I'm on the Jersey Turnpike. See you at 9 a.m." And yet, it never bothered me. I was first and foremost accountable to myself. I had goals I wanted to achieve, and to achieve them, I needed to be busy. I held myself responsible for booking full days of promising appointments Monday through Friday. All day, every day. So, when I got the call, it wasn't a problem. There were no worries, scrambling or extra stress.

Over the years, I learned to enjoy these days most of all. It was great having someone in the car to talk with all day. We learned together. Rob got to know many of my clients and was instrumental in many early sales. Along the way, I taught Rob some of my rules for working hard and playing hard. You see, I always thought it was important to find little rewards along the way.

When you start most days early in the morning and are out on the road all day, you often find you need a little boost by around 3 p.m. I showed Rob the value of a Wendy's Frosty. That little mix of chocolate and sugar rush would be just the thing to keep us going.

Some of my peers never understood the importance of managing their schedule this way, with full days of appointments set up. Many found having their supervisor ride with them stressful, and they would cancel when they didn't have full days planned. Too often, they wouldn't take responsibility to have enough work planned on their own.

I learned:

> Simply plan each day as if your supervisor is going to call you at 7 a.m. and tell you they're on their way.

Flash forward about twenty-five years, and you would still find me working hard every day. But it was now *work*. It was no longer play. A lot of changes at Clipper and a final acquisition by a large company, one more concerned about quarterly profit statements than people or clients, had taken the passion out of my daily routine. By this time, several people I worked with closely were approaching retirement, and like them, I dreamed of no longer working. No more daily grind. I'd had enough. Now, in my mid-fifties, I would sometimes wonder if it was simply my age—maybe I no longer had the stamina or desire for that extra mile. Maybe I had stretched myself as far as I could.

Well, I can tell you now: No, I was not too old. No, I was not done stretching. I simply had to find the play again. I worked on this book for several months. I started a new sales training business. I have been networking and collaborating with dozens of new contacts.

I have been working harder than I have in five years. But it is no longer *work*. I now *play* five (sometimes six) days a week. I went from experiencing what I called "Sunday depression" (anxiety about another Monday approaching) to anxiously awaiting my Monday mornings.

Work hard and play hard go hand in hand. When you are happy and fulfilled in your work, play comes naturally.

SLOW SPEED BUMP **Spend a few minutes** reflecting on these questions, then add your thoughts to your notes.

- What aspects of your job do you find most enjoyable?
- List two or three productive habits you can add to your week that may seem more like play to you. Can they help you achieve more success?
- How might you stretch yourself to reach a goal?
- Dream about your next vacation. What goal will allow you to enjoy that experience if you achieved it first?
- Are your days planned to be full of sales appointments and key meetings? If not, what daily habit can you begin to create more full days?
- Do you have a good work/life balance? If not, what changes might you need to consider?

Do not wear yourself out to get rich.

Proverbs 23:4a

Day Eleven
The Big Ask

I HAVE ALWAYS BELIEVED in shooting for the moon, and I was fortunate to have enough confidence to set aside any doubts and simply stretch for my goals. You can't succeed unless you try.

To shoot for the moon or aim for any lofty goal, you have to focus on it, know what you want, and then take action. Sometimes, that means asking for things that seem too much or too big. Yet some of the biggests shots we take begin with the biggest asks.

While this wasn't always the best idea, I have always believed in the "Big Ask."

When I was a freshman in high school, I remember being angry and disappointed when I asked my parents for permission to play football and they refused. Looking back, the fact that I was only 4'11" and about ninety-five pounds means they probably saved me several injuries and tears.

I fell in love at first sight when I started a new job in the fall of '83. It was my first day at the Shop Rite grocery store on Route 70 in Marlton, New Jersey. I got that job after leaving a management position at a local McDonald's, where I had worked for a little over a year. I quit after asking for and being denied a 25¢ per hour raise. I was nineteen years old and attending college full time. I left when my Big Ask received a "no" response to start a new job pushing shopping carts and loading groceries, even though it was for less money.

Despite the bruising my ego received, I soon learned that even when our Big Ask is refused, it's not the worst thing in the world. Sometimes, better things await us.

You see, I met my future wife, Kelly, that first day at my new job. But several months and multiple attempts to speak with her passed before we actually had our first date. She finally agreed to go with me to a party one Saturday night after work. It was a Big Ask for me, and at the time she didn't know that I had to scramble before picking her up that evening since I had to plan, organize and prepare a party for her to attend. That hastily prepared party and Big Ask were the beginning of our courtship and led to the Biggest Ask of my life, eventually asking Kelly to be my wife.

A few years later, I stopped going to college after taking classes for about four years. I had been excited to be a freshman at Temple University in Philadelphia in the fall of '82. Things changed for me a semester later, when I transferred to Rutgers University in Camden, New Jersey. The experience of college never matched how I felt while working. I quit altogether despite achieving about ninety credits toward my bachelor's degree. I always regretted this decision later in life, but at the time I was young, naïve and blind to the value of attending classes. I was studying accounting while being fortunate enough to work full time for a local accounting firm. What I was being taught in school failed to line up with what was actually being done in the field. So, I lost interest and took a shot at the business world.

That accounting job led me to a satisfying career at a young age. The firm's owner was a partner in a postsecondary vocational school. I began working for both the accounting firm and the school and eventually became a director of one of the school's campuses while still in my mid-twenties. I was directing a school in Kingston, Pennsylvania, when I made my next Big Ask. I asked for the opportunity to open new campuses for the school in Scranton and Allentown, Pennsylvania. Kelly and I were married by this time with two very young children, but my Big Asks were still not done.

When I realized that all my efforts and accomplishments with the school weren't going to yield the financial rewards I hoped for, I eagerly volunteered when the opportunity came up to help them start an advertising company, where my income potential was much higher. I had no knowledge, background or skills in advertising sales. I was leaving a secure position for a complete unknown, even though I had never thought of myself as a salesperson. If you're thinking Kelly must have been a saint, you would be correct.

I said at the start of this chapter, I have always had the confidence simply to set aside my doubts and stretch myself. That confidence only existed because of the love and patience of those around me. It started with my mom and continued with my wife. I would not have achieved any of my successes without the confidence they instilled in me.

As you may have guessed, I loved advertising sales. With only about nine months of experience in the field, the local sales manager for Clipper Magazine tried to recruit me. I was intrigued because they were one of the premier ad magazines in the area. While I did consider the recruitment offer, I turned it down because I didn't see enough growth potential in that market.

I will never forget the day shortly after I started selling ads for our school program when my grandmother called. She had just received a Clipper mailing and was frantically asking if I had seen it and how I could possibly compete. To some extent, she was correct. I soon realized that the best path for me would be to take a closer look at Clipper.

A few months later, I made one of my biggest Asks up to that point. I garnered a meeting with the founders of Clipper in their Lancaster, Pennsylvania, office. I asked if they would consider hiring me and allowing me to open the state of New Jersey for them. Kelly and I had determined we would be moving back to her hometown of Marlton to live and raise our kids. So we took a shot, and Clipper said yes. They agreed to pay me about half of what I had been earning in my last position, but Kelly and I saw a bright future.

Throughout my life, I have taken the shot, but with each shot, there has always been a Big Ask. You won't always get what you ask for. Often, the shots you take won't work out as you hope. But I have always believed, as American pastor and author Norman Vincent Peale said:

> Shoot for the moon. Even if you miss it, you will still land among the stars.

I have enjoyed a fulfilling life and sales career among those stars, and I know I landed there only because I consistently chose to shoot for the moon.

A close friend of mine and a former coworker at Clipper, Jimmy Drevs, always used to say, "Tell a story, make a point." Well, I have told a few stories here, so now it is time to make a few points.

My first point is that there are many ways to ask a big question. When asked a simple yes or no question, how often do you err on the side of "no"? Many people are afraid to say "yes" because they may make a mistake or regret that "yes" at some point. Sometimes, they will say "no" because they want to exercise some control over things.

When you ask a question, especially a Big Ask, never offer a simple yes or no answer. In sales, it is crucial to give a business owner or decision maker an opportunity to exercise control, a way not to feel sold. It is always good to lead them down a road where the only sensible answer is a "yes."

I have spent a lot of time cold calling prospects, contacting people who weren't expecting a sales call. I would go from business to business knocking on doors or make phone calls, hoping to get a store owner to agree to an appointment. I learned that simply asking for a "yes" to an appointment might lead to several objections why they couldn't set one. Success came more often when I got any objections out of the way at the start.

- What time of day are you usually free for a few minutes?
- Of the things I have shown you, which is most valuable to you?

- What is the biggest struggle for your business today?
- Do you have a strategy to overcome that struggle?

With answers to questions like these out of the way, I would now ask for the appointment. I might say something like, "I have helped a few other business owners with the same struggle. How about if I stop by tomorrow around 1 p.m. and drop off a few of the ads those businesses have used? Will you be here? Great! If it turns out you have a few minutes, I can tell you more about how they used the ads and the results they got."

Based on their answers, which weren't just "yes" or "no," I pitched an appointment that simply made sense. It didn't leave room for fear to get in their way, but instead promised a potential solution to their problem.

My second point here is about providing options. Continuing the example from above, when I booked that appointment, I would ensure I had a strong presentation by planning and preparing for that meeting. I would spend time in the meeting fact-finding. My goal would be that as we continued to talk, I would develop a solution for that business owner's specific problem. Now, here's the key.

How do I present the solution and ask for the sale? Yes or no questions aren't any better in this situation. In fact, when you ask for a sale, an actual investment of money, they are even riskier. People fear making a mistake or of "being sold." So, you must up your game if you are going to take a shot.

I always liked to provide options in my Ask. Proposing two or three options doesn't offer an easy "no" for an answer. It also allows a decision maker to exercise some control. Our goal is for them to make a decision that is ultimately a "yes," but feels like a solution they chose, not something they were sold.

This is where shooting for the moon comes in. Once I developed a strong solution for a business owner, I would offer a couple of options for addressing their specific needs. I would recommend the large commitment (the Big Ask) and explain that I would understand if they weren't ready for that—if they needed to start smaller and build up more trust in me and my product. I would then show them a less expensive solution and explain this was what most of my clients started with. Then I would ask which they felt comfortable doing today. I led them to choose an option, not answer "yes" or "no." I showed them a large exciting solution as well as giving them a very acceptable popular option. They were in control.

I prospered for over twenty-eight years selling Clipper ads to a wide variety of business owners, many of whom were clients for several years. I could not have achieved that without providing reasonable and effective solutions. Often, the Big Ask solution would ultimately work best for a client, but it took time for some of them to feel comfortable investing at that level, and that was okay.

After my position at Clipper was eliminated, I began a new career as a sales trainer. This was a major transition for me. I could no longer simply drive up to a prospect and knock on their door. Instead, my prospecting efforts are now spent on LinkedIn and writing compelling emails. Today, a Big Ask is convincing a large media company to simply have a Zoom call with me.

Believe in and make your Big Ask.

Luckily for me, the same fundamentals that proved successful in my door-to-door days still work. I only have to tweak them for selling online. Having options is still valuable, and I use them daily. I haven't had to change how I set appointments. Offering a face-to-face visit, a Zoom meeting, or providing a walk-thru of the services on my website via a phone call all have their place. Bringing value to each encounter and being prepared to put on a good show when they agree to an appointment are still necessities.

When you shoot for the moon, whether you land on it or among the stars, it must be a win for everyone. Work hard, formulate a proposal that makes sense for everyone, be confident... and then take the shot.

SLOW SPEED BUMP

Spend a few minutes reflecting on these questions, then add your thoughts to your notes.

- What is your normal Big Ask in your sales job?
- What options do you offer instead of simply asking yes/no questions? If none, what options could you begin offering?
- Think about some of your best sales stories. Do you have a strong point to make following each story? What point could you make to help move the sale along?
- Do you have a Big Ask related to your career that you'd like to make? Are you shooting for the moon in your career? What might you begin doing to best position and prepare yourself for that Ask?

But when you ask, you must believe and not doubt, because the one who doubts is like a wave of the sea, blown and tossed by the wind.

James 1:6

Day Twelve
It's the Little Things

IN EVERYTHING YOU DO, there is a fine line between winning and losing; between success and failure; between reaching the moon, falling among the stars, and never getting off the ground. For me, it's not the big things I do that make a difference, but the accumulated effect of all the little things I do—those little everyday details so many often overlook.

I need to cover a few little things that made a big difference when going for a Big Ask. These four factors may be just what your next Big Ask needs.

- Feel, Felt, Found
- Keep it simple, stupid (KISS)
- Build trust
- Practice before big calls

The concept of Feel, Felt, Found was especially helpful for my Clipper sales. When business owners gave me an objection, explaining why they didn't want to buy from me, I told them, "I understand how you *feel*. I have had several other clients who *felt* the same way at first. Let me show you what they *found*." By verbalizing these three components while showing off beautiful sample ads, it allowed me to tailor my presentation specifically for them.

This simple concept allowed me to acknowledge that their objection was worthy. I didn't become argumentative, since I knew I could never win by disagreeing and fighting with them. By acknowledging that other clients I had worked with had felt the same way, it allowed me to show them I had solved the problem for other business owners. I was demonstrating expertise that should interest them, building trust instead of building up barriers. I was presenting a solution to their dilemma—one proven to work for others.

Imagine speaking with a small local sub shop owner. They explain to you they don't think they can afford to buy an ad. You reply you understand how they feel, saying something like, "Let me show you an ad I did for XYZ Sub Shop in the next town over. The owner there felt the same way as you. He didn't feel he could afford it when I first met with him. What he found was that he received far more traffic and even a higher average sale from the customers who came from my ad. He also saw results for a much longer time from it. My ad actually ended up being much more cost-effective than the cheaper ads he had been running elsewhere that weren't nearly as effective."

A presentation like this, combined with displaying a few beautiful sample ads always made a profound statement, especially if it came with a referral and compelling story that addressed their objection.

If you were excitedly thinking the next item in today's list, KISS, was about the rock band, I apologize. "I Was Made For

Lovin' You" is powerful, but not nearly as important as the concept "Keep It Simple, Stupid." First coined by the US Navy in 1960, the KISS principle states that most things work best if we keep them simple. The more complicated they become, the more likely they are to fail. The same concept applies to sales. It's straightforward, yet I constantly see examples of people making things more complicated than they need to be.

If you are asking something and the person you are talking to doesn't understand the question, that is a problem. Simplify what you're saying. Otherwise, you probably won't get the answer you're hoping for. For many people, it's not always easy to make things simple. If you are constantly being rejected or not getting the answer you are looking for, stop and look at how you are presenting the options. If it is something you believe most reasonable people would agree to, then your problem may very well be that your delivery is too complicated. Try a new approach—and please keep it simple, stupid.

If you are making a Big Ask, you better have established some trust first. This is one of the little touches so many miss. The concept is to demonstrate the value of what you have to offer, as I covered a few days ago. Always show them something new, something from your materials you haven't shown them before. Tired of hearing "no"? Showing value over time is a little thing that builds trust. And when you have built that trust, you will have more confidence in your Big Ask.

I have had great success after numerous visits to a prospect because I would bring value and new ideas each time. I was consistent and showed that I was reliable and hard working.

Then I could make a Big Ask and frame it with a "Trust me. This will work for you."

Look someone in the eyes and ask them to trust you, but only after you have spent time earning it. That can be huge. Some prospects might feel guilty, while others took pity on me but appreciated the effort. Does it work every time? Absolutely not. Some people never feel guilty and are slow to trust. But it *never* works if you haven't done the little things that build trust.

Finally, let's talk about practice. I don't know about you, but for me, it didn't matter how long I had been doing sales presentations. My first couple of calls in a day were seldom my best. The more calls I made and the more I presented, the stronger I got. Hit me with a tough objection first thing on Monday morning, and I would leave without a sale. Hit me with that same objection later in the afternoon, and I would pull out a sales contract.

If you are like me, then do what I did. Any morning when I had an important presentation to make, I would always schedule a few cold calls beforehand. If I had a 9:30 a.m. appointment with that sub shop owner and knew they'd possibly be signing today, I would stop on my way and make three or four cold calls. They gave me the practice I needed to align my thoughts and sharpen and focus my mind.

Sometimes, those cold calls would turn into something. I could then schedule a set appointment to come back all because of name-dropping the shop down the street I had an appointment with.

Yesterday, I asked you to take shots and shoot for the moon. Taking shots will enable you to succeed. Have you ever watched any successful professional athlete not warm up before a game? Don't they shoot a few free throws? Don't they take batting practice or shoot a couple of pucks at the net? If you want to take more shots, spend more time practicing.

Why is it so few people do all the little things? I believe it's because many of the little things have no immediate impact. We all want to see a quick return on investment. We want to know the little things really will work. The problem is that proof is rarely visible, especially if you aren't sure where to look for it.

I prided myself on the magazine I was producing, especially the edition mailed in my town. I worked extra hard to make sure it had all the right ingredients, and other Clipper salespeople would often use it as a valuable sample in their own markets. Cherry Hill, New Jersey, was a thriving area in the mid-'90s. It was home to some of the finest upscale mom-and-pop retailers anywhere in the state. I showcased an amazing group of quality retail advertisers in almost every issue I published, and several jewelry stores advertised with us for all their major sales.

There was one jewelry store in particular, however, that I could never get to work with me. I was a very persistent seller, though, and this jewelry store was in a shopping center where I already had several clients, only a short distance from my home. I tried many times to earn their business. After a couple years, my efforts had decreased to only an occasional visit, since I could see they weren't well received. But then, I got a phone call from the owner, asking me to stop in and speak with him.

I didn't know this at the time, but he had recently read an article about coupon promotions in a trusted jewelry trade publication. He asked his employees which coupon magazine, if any,

Earn trust before you ask for it.

they liked. They all enthusiastically mentioned my Clipper. That day, the business owner signed an annual commitment with me and became my favorite and strongest jewelry store client for several years. It was all the little things I had been doing for years to make my magazine stand out that made this sale happen.

It is so easy to look across the street and see greener grass, to see a land of opportunity so much better than what you have today. It is easier to make excuses for what you lack, than it is to do all that extra work. But it's all in the little things. As our church pastor likes to say:

> The grass is not greener across the street. The grass is greener where it is watered.

Today, I have covered only a few of the seemingly little things that can help you. Whatever product you are selling or sales process you use, I promise there are little things you need to focus on that will create results in time.

To grow my sales training business and build quality prospects, I need to spend time almost daily on LinkedIn. After researching best practices, I have learned several little things I must do to succeed. I don't always see an immediate return from thoughtful posts offering valuable content or receive a response from connections as I engage with their posts, but it's worth the time and effort to do. I have also spent time learning how to tape, edit and post video content, so I can create my own valuable content. All these little things, done over time, have helped bring on new clients, but they don't deliver right away.

Build a daily habit of doing the little things, and you will ultimately see them affect your life.

SLOW SPEED BUMP

Spend a few minutes reflecting on these questions, then add your thoughts to your notes.

- What are the little things you should be doing regularly?

- How can you use Feel, Felt, Found in your sales process?

- In what ways are you building trust with your prospects?

- What habits can you add that will build even more trust with them?

- Should you simplify your calls, emails, presentations, etc.? If so, how will you do that?

- List several prospects who have seemed to stall or are stuck. What materials haven't you shown that might help rekindle their interest?

Day Thirteen
There Are No Perfect People

I F YOU WAIT FOR A PERFECT TIME, for that one perfect piece needed to begin, for the perfect materials for your presentation, for the perfect words to say... it will probably be too late.

In an article for The Economist, Dan Montano once wrote:

> Every morning in Africa, a gazelle wakes up. It knows it must run faster than the fastest lion or it will be killed. Every morning a lion wakes up. It knows it must outrun the slowest gazelle or it will starve to death. It doesn't matter whether you are a lion or a gazelle: when the sun comes up, you'd better be running.

And organization development practitioner Eva Young once said:

> To think too long about doing a thing often becomes its undoing.

How many great ideas have you had that came undone as you considered them? And considered them. And...

When I left a stable position in education for a start-up advertising division with a brand-new product, it seemed like a great idea. And luckily for me, I started running.

The owner of the chain of schools I worked for brought in one of his favorite ad sales reps. She had been selling him ad space for a while, and he trusted her expertise. She gave me and a few others a one-day crash course in ad sales. I wasn't particularly good after that one day, but I kept running.

While transitioning into this new role, I still had an executive assistant working with me. She handled my schedule and ran our office. Each day for the first several weeks, I would arrive back in that office at the close of business to check in. I would hand her a stack of business cards I had collected and let her know which ones she should expect a call from.

I can still recall one particular afternoon. As I handed her the cards I had collected that day and excitedly told her about one of my cold calls, I could see a strange smile on her face. When I asked about it, she laughed and then exclaimed, "Tom, they never call you back."

She was so right. In my excitement, I was overlooking cold reality. No matter what a business owner told me during my visit, they never had any plans to call me back. I was far from perfect... but I kept running.

Then, one day, an amazing thing happened for me. I had an appointment with the franchise owner of Little Caesar's Pizza in Scranton, Pennsylvania. I made my usual sales presentation while she and I sat in the small vestibule of their waiting area. I'm not even sure why, but I made a Big Ask. We still had the front cover available for our premiere issue. Actually, we had almost all our pages available. The front cover was our most expensive location, yet I offered it to her and without much hesitation, she agreed. She even bought it at the full price, which I wasn't expecting ever to get.

Still excited from what was then my largest ever sale, I sold another full-page ad the next day to a local auto parts store. I didn't suddenly have a fantastic presentation. In fact, I was still far from perfect. I learned later this auto parts store advertised in all the direct mail they could and that Little Caesar's Pizza owners are encouraged to grab all the front and back covers they can in direct mail. Those types of ads are almost always a home run for their franchisees. I was still far from perfect, but that didn't matter when my prospects could see past my efforts and understand the value of my product.

Well, our first edition did premiere. And while those two sales accounted for over 80 percent of the total revenue we collected, we were off and, you guessed it... running. I would continue to learn, in sales and life, that you cannot wait to be perfect. You will never achieve perfection. You simply need to keep running, keep trying, keep growing and keep learning. Who knows what may have happened if I hadn't gotten those two appointments, had I been afraid to call on them, fearing I wasn't ready yet?

Thirty years later, I understand I had found my true calling. I am thankful I didn't miss the opportunity by waiting and that I knew enough to thirst for more knowledge. I would grow and benefit from learning. Understanding you are not and never will be perfect opens you up to wanting to learn and grow. Despite making many mistakes in my early career, my hard work and willingness to laugh at and learn from those mistakes propelled me.

Don't wait for perfection—give it your best shot now.

There are a few ways you can "keep running" while making mistakes, learning and growing stronger. I learned quickly that sales only happened when I had an appointment to make a presentation. It was rare to make a sale on a cold call since it normally took a detailed and strong presentation full of sample ads, an array of fact-finding probing questions, the creation of a solution, and finally a negotiation. Since my goal was to make sales daily, I learned I would need to wake up each day with a few promising appointments set. The problem was, setting appointments with busy, hard-to-reach business owners is much easier said than done. I needed to find ways to set more of them.

I discovered the "art of assumed appointments." If I had all the ingredients necessary for an actual appointment by having asked revealing questions earlier, I could book an assumed appointment on my own.

If I had a scheduled appointment in a town on Thursday morning, I would review my prospects and find a couple located nearby, ones with decision makers who were typically in on Thursday mornings. I would then review what I needed and prepare as if they had also set an appointment for that day. Most times, after a cold call, an owner would tell me to follow up in a week or two. I would drop by on that Thursday morning, prepared for an appointment, and explain that I was following up as requested and had brought several things to show them. Before asking if they had time or wanted to see me (they might not), I would present the ideas I had prepared for them—showing value. Of course, this method doesn't work every time. However, it does work quite often. Even when they didn't have enough time, our conversation would often lead them to book an actual appointment on a day when they were available. This is only one basic example, but it illustrates the concept of looking for ways to keep running effectively, even when there may not seem to be any.

I also used another approach that illustrates this throughout my career in sales, which I called the "expanding bullseye approach." Sample ads were my strongest tool during a presentation. If I was calling on a Dunkin' franchise owner, you can imagine the power of a few actual successful ads from other Dunkin' stores. Perfect, right? Well, they would be, but usually I only had a few other Dunkin' stores to approach in my territory. When I was dealing with anyone other than Dunkin', I had successful sample ads, but there wasn't a perfect business to share them with. Actual Dunkin' stores would have been a bullseye. However, those sample ads could work almost as well with other doughnut or coffee shops. These prospects were within the target area, slightly outside the center—just off the bullseye. When shown the success from the actual Dunkin' ad, it wasn't much of a stretch for a different store to see value in them. Again, great sample ad, but only a few prospects I could show it to.

I learned over time that I needed to extrapolate from my successful prospecting to find new businessses that covered a few more rings outside the bullseye. Those same successful sample ads from Dunkin' were strong ads to show many other small businesses. I could use them in bagel stores and small sandwich shops. Mom-and-pop ice cream or frozen yogurt stores could relate. A local bakery could see the value. The key is that while the Dunkin' sample may not have been perfect for a local bakery, combined with a good story, it was more than enough. Take what works for you and keep running with it. Confidently sharing successes and being enthusiastic gets people excited and grabs their attention, not perfection.

I worked with far too many sales reps who would start on a presentation to their local bakery without any sample ads. They only felt comfortable presenting the perfect ad.

Some people say you need to "act as if" you are successful to become successful. For many, this is difficult, as it often seems misleading or inauthentic. To me, it is far more about just keeping at it, being open to new ideas, and constantly learning and growing, but also staying in motion; never stopping or stalling until you have it figured out. If you don't try, how will you ever succeed?

Contemplate the activities you have been avoiding, the sales you aren't attempting because something doesn't yet feel right, and the conversations you have been thinking about for far too long. Open yourself up to mistakes and to learning. Keep running and watch things happen.

SLOW SPEED BUMP **Spend a few minutes** reflecting on these questions, then add your thoughts to your notes.

- What steps in your sales process slow you down?
- Are there any effective, though not perfect, ways to speed them up?
- What perfect opportunities have you been waiting on that you may be ready to begin now?
- Is there a prospect you would love to approach but haven't felt ready for? What is stopping you?

Day Fourteen
Ready, Set, Go

IF READING THIS BOOK EVERY DAY is motivating you the
way I hope, then it is inspiring you to *go*! You've probably
long since left *ready* and *set* behind and have already added a
few new daily habits into your routine. When I tell you it is time
to discuss proper planning and preparation, you may be a little
bewildered. "Didn't we start with planning? I've been at this
for two weeks already," you're thinking. "What did I miss?"

Don't worry, you haven't missed anything. And I hope you
are ready for the crucial next step toward success.

During my days as VP of Sales at Clipper, I spent a good part
of my time developing and presenting the training materials for
our new hire programs. We had a practice I was a big fan of.
Once hired, a new sales rep would complete their introduction
to the company and initial sales training in their home territory,
supported by their sales manager. They would then spend eight
to twelve weeks prospecting and would need to make a few sales
before being invited to attend our formal training program.
Once invited, they would make the trip to our corporate office

in Lancaster, Pennsylvania. Here, they would spend a week in comprehensive classroom training.

We believed that much of the intense sales training we provided would be lost if given too soon and without any context. We simply don't know what we don't know. We need to struggle and hit a few brick walls before we can appreciate the techniques that will get through them. We wanted our new hires to spend their training week with light bulbs flashing on each day.

It is now Day Fourteen of your journey. I hope you can see your path developing and that you genuinely believe you can control your journey and manage yourself to success. Now it's time to discuss how it all begins with proper planning and preparation.

Whatever goals you have set for your business, to succeed, you need to:

- sell to more new clients
- keep your old clients

This may seem pretty basic, and it *is* a simple concept. Even if your goal is to build new relationships while keeping the existing ones strong, planning and preparation are the best way to achieve it. The key is to work hard at it, and put the time in.

Now you may be thinking, "I understood that several days ago. This isn't new." Congratulations! You have been paying attention.

But pay closer attention today. Don't mistake the minor success of the sales you've made thus far for a complete mastery of sales techniques. As I have said, you must learn constantly. It's time to build on the knowledge and success you have gained.

Start by building a roadmap for each new prospect. The key to success when signing new clients and keeping existing business strong is to treat every company as unique.

Every company, like every individual, has different needs, goals, likes and dislikes. A cookie-cutter approach will get you some sales, but it will not lead you to long-term success. That is where the roadmap comes in.

They say the quickest way to get from point A to point B is a straight line. In sales, it's not about the quickest route to point B. It is about ensuring you get there. You need to build a roadmap in which you are prepared for every dead end, traffic jam, one-way street, and road closure—understanding all the while that the map for client A will probably differ greatly from the one for client B. So, how do you properly build such a roadmap to success?

First, identify the many objections you have faced in the past and expect them to arise again today. Then, prepare the materials, talking points and stories you will need to move past those objections. Next, ask probing questions designed to get a glimpse of the road you may need to travel for this client.

Many salespeople take the scenic route, enjoying the view and a conversation free of objections and issues—only to be disappointed when they never arrive at their destination.

I was fortunate to keep many of my personal Clipper clients for years. Why? Because I was never afraid to ask the tough questions. After each ad was mailed, I would inquire as to how it

Build a unique roadmap for each prospect.

had performed. Which coupons were working? How did they feel about the ad?

It was difficult to convince sales reps of the value of these questions when they believed that no news is good news. As a sales manager, I wasn't very understanding when a rep told me they had lost a long-time client because the ads were no longer working. It was easier for them to blame the ads' results than to blame themselves.

Nope. I would not buy that. I wanted to understand how they had let it get to that point. They should have seen the road construction weeks earlier and found an alternate route for their client.

Always be on the lookout for road signs, especially those warning of danger. If you plan and prepare for changes in your roadmap, you will find solutions. Sales and relationship-building are almost always a matter of presenting a solution that someone needs and showing them a plan to achieve it. Build a solution and close the sale. It doesn't matter which road got you there, so long as it works for that individual.

As well as preparing to overcome objections, plan ways to interact more often with the people you need to see. Building strong relationships is all about quality touches that create those opportunities I mentioned early on, where you create your own luck.

Preparing quality touches is a matter of three things:

- having the right approach
- sharing the right materials
- being there at the right time

I have covered these to a degree already, but I haven't explained how proper planning gets you there.

Having the right approach is all about understanding the person or business you hope to connect with, knowing what they care about and what their goals are, and understanding what problems they are facing or what may interest them. A comprehensive, customized approach will be a catalyst for more quality touches.

When the quality touch happens, do you have the materials to make the best use of their time and attention? Have you prepared and brought the materials to move the sale along the road today? Most of us have a finite number of prospects we hope to connect with in a given week or cycle. That means it only takes a little preparation to have the materials with you always.

It's important to note that sometimes opportunity knocks when you don't expect it. Never be afraid to say you don't have an answer to something or that you don't have what you need today.

Sometimes, a prospect fell into my lap. I have had meetings with a client in a diner, during which a business owner came up to say they had overheard our conversation and wanted to ask a question. (Yes, I talk a little loud sometimes!) I would always explain to them, "I can show you this ad, but I have some great ones I would love to show you and will bring to our next visit."

You never know when the right time will occur. As you discovered earlier, you always should be looking for ways to have luck on your side at the right time. Plan for each roadmap to be filled with quality touches, using all the three V's of value. Understand the importance of being in front of a prospect at just the right moment.

Make a daily habit of looking ahead and preparing the right approaches for the right prospects, accompanied by the right materials. Then, when the right time comes, you will be prepared.

I told you earlier about meeting my future wife, Kelly, and how it was love at first sight for me. Our first date happened because I asked her to accompany me to a party. But what I didn't mention was all the time and effort I spent on the quality touches that got me there.

Kelly was working part-time evenings in the bakery department at the Shop Rite where I worked. Each night when I noticed her working, I would make sure I walked past that department whenever possible. I also got in the habit of stopping by on my nightly break to buy a cup of hot tea. Every break I frequented the bakery was an opportunity for me to approach and engage with her, an opportunity for me to build trust and rapport. Had I not made these many touches over a period of several weeks, she might not have accepted that party invitation. But I was ready. I was set. And I just had to wait for the right time to go!

Kelly and I host a sales podcast, *OK Boomer, Teach Me Sales,* where we share stories, tips and best practices in sales and leadership. The show's premise is that the behaviors, skills and traits for success haven't changed over the years. What made someone successful thirty years ago or even longer back remain fundamental to achieving success today. We also show how the way we communicate those fundamentals has changed.

I am very thankful that I met my wife at a time when my right approach with the right materials at the right time could be communicated face-to-face. Had she been able to merely "swipe left" on her phone, I'm sure my life would have been far more difficult.

Technology, the internet and social media have transformed the way people live. They have also majorly affected how to plan and prepare. When it comes to sales, social media is often what separates the good from the great today.

I am convinced that if communication back in the '90s had been more like it is today, I would have stayed in sales and not transitioned into management. Going the extra mile with planning and preparation was my thing. I would spend many nights looking through countless issues of Clipper from across the country. I would build file after file of the ads I swiped. ("Swiping" is what we called the process of selecting an ad sample to show, cutting it out of a magazine, and filing it in a collection to share during a sales presentation. This is similar to how research is done online today, whether for copy or images.)

If I had a major appointment with a furniture store owner, I sometimes had to look through dozens of magazines for suitable ads to show them. I had to learn which area magazines typically had which kinds of ads. What if I'd only had to do an internet search for "furniture ads" and they were instantly there, ready to print?

I often spent hours driving in my territory, visiting stores in fact-finding mode. I would walk in, wait and then spend five to ten minutes chatting with a clerk. My goal was to ask enough revealing questions while the owner was out to develop a roadmap for the day when they were in.

Sometimes, after several of these trips, I would unearth the fact that the business was busy planning an upcoming event.

When that happened, I couldn't wait to follow up when I could catch the owner, bringing just the right sample ads for the event they were planning. What if I could just sit on my couch and see a social media post from that business announcing their upcoming event?

If I was helping a start-up social media company, I could search for every suitable prospect for that company on Facebook and like their pages. Daily, I could review their posts and look for opportunities to discuss with our prospects. The posts might include things like possible openings for a discussion, reasons to explain why I am calling them, and anything else they're promoting right now. This is a great way to establish those quality touches.

When I think back on all the time and effort I spent planning and preparing, then realize how much more efficiently I could do all of that today... I tell you, I probably wouldn't be writing this book. I would be selling more ads. Probably while relaxing somewhere.

When I imagine how customized and personal I could make every greeting, every quality touch, I get a little depressed because, every day, I see salespeople and business leaders not using these valuable tools. Seeking creative ways to develop a connection with your prospects is a fundamental that hasn't changed over time. Even though how you build a strong roadmap has changed, the effort needed to build it has not.

After the past two weeks, I hope you are ready to understand this chapter and put it effectively into place. Take a few minutes and detail all the ways you can use today's technology to improve your approach, your materials, and even your timing.

Need help exploring your options? There are countless talented and helpful people on every social media platform, offering free content to get you started. Not sure where to turn? Connect with me on LinkedIn, then send me a message asking for help.

SLOW SPEED BUMP **Spend a few minutes** reflecting on these questions, then add your thoughts to your notes.

- What daily habits have you begun that are showing an impact for you?
- What daily habits should you implement?
- Are there any dead-ends you routinely face? What unique approach to solving them can you try?
- Which tough questions should you start asking?
- Are you making enough quality touches? How can you make these a daily habit?

Day Fifteen
An Attitude of Gratitude

FORMER US SUPREME COURT JUSTICE Thurgood Marshall said:

> None of us has gotten where we are solely by pulling ourselves up by our own bootstraps. We got here because somebody bent down and helped us.

My wife, Kelly, wakes up and starts every day with the same prayer. She asks the Lord to let her be a blessing to someone today.

Spend a few minutes thinking about those who have bent down to help you. Those that have helped shape and build your confidence in what you do. Then consider how you might express your gratitude to them. You can only manage yourself to success when you acknowledge and appreciate others and their impact on your life, your journey, and your success.

For two weeks now, I have talked about confidence. We must all find confidence in ourselves. It must come from somewhere, and is usually instilled in you by someone. For me, it all began with the amazing love shown to me by my mom, Sharon. I could afford to be confident and take chances, to make mistakes and learn from them. This was because my mom always had my back. I knew that, no matter what, she would always be there for me. She always believed in me. I can never properly express how grateful I am for her love.

Kelly and I often joke as we reminisce about our life together. I tell her she now lives with Tom 2.0—which is a good thing, because Tom 1.0 was not the easiest person to live with. I was driven, obsessed with success, and far too self-centered. All that while, we lived paycheck to paycheck and raised two kids. After my mom, Kelly has always been my biggest supporter. She has seen me at my weakest moments and has always been encouraging.

It is easier to shoot for the moon when you know someone will be there after every miss, no matter how low the next fall may be.

I have reached this point in my life because so many have bent down to help me along the way. I realized in writing this book that I, unfortunately, skip the Acknowledgments upon finishing most books, the part where the author thanks those who have helped them along the way. I encourage you to read mine when you get there. It's my way of expressing my gratitude to just a few of the people who have given me so much.

I hope you spend time today building an attitude focused on sharing your gratitude. Send an email or text message to someone who's been on your mind. Has a story or thought about someone come into your thoughts recently? Let them know. Don't let such thoughts be seldom spoken.

Once you have built your attitude of gratitude, I hope you will be encouraged and find true joy in becoming a person who seeks to help others. You have amazing gifts, gifts that can help someone in need. Seek them out. Be of service to someone today.

If you are concerned about keeping your best clients, you need to care so much that you are afraid to lose them. When you fear losing them, you will take the necessary steps to retain them.

Don't be complacent. Instead, focus on these four fundamental factors in keeping your clients:

- Stay in touch.
- Share the pain.
- Align with their needs by encouraging creativity.
- Make it about more than money.

Start by staying in touch. Communication is essential. You may not always have all the answers, but the people important to you need to hear from you. Those most important to us (sometimes our biggest clients) are often overlooked because they seem self-sufficient. Instead, treat them as if they were the most vulnerable. Take no one for granted. Getting out there and communicating is your most important job.

Your team, your clients, even your best friends will probably go through pain at some point. Beyond job performance or sales return on investment, a personal crisis can affect an individual client or team member. When they are worried about things outside your control, your deadlines and needs will not be their biggest concern. You need to show them you are there for them. Be a part of the solution, not another problem to handle. It's not enough just to say you're there for them. Share their pain by finding ways to alleviate it for them, and sometimes that's going to mean taking on some of it yourself by deferring an ad, taking on additional responsibilities, completing a task, or some other sacrifice that helps them out.

If you are a sales rep, business owner or leader, you probably don't spend a lot of time in the weeds with your clients. There are times, however, when you may need to get dirty and spend time with someone in the trenches. I have known sales reps who would jump behind a counter when a valued business owner was swamped and needed help. You won't always have all the answers, but people will know they can rely on you and that you care.

Empower prospects and clients to share ideas about how they plan to implement your product or service and what they hope to accomplish. Help them envision their future with the successful partnership you're creating together. Being aligned with others will be successful only if they feel and see that alignment.

Who are your top clients? Spend a few minutes considering how you can empower them and work closer together. Find ways of including them in your decision making. Help bring their ideas into focus.

Want to help reduce stress in those you work with? Encourage their creativity. We all struggle when things are out of our control. Give your clients opportunities to be more in control. Work with them to learn how they can grow and develop. Empower them to seek new avenues to drive traffic for their business, improve sales, increase earnings, or simply find more joy. Help others reinvent themselves or even their role in your life. As they find more ways to engage and be creative with you, they will naturally align with you and will be happier and more excited about their time with you.

Make working with you about more than money. If people only work with you or for you to earn an income, you are not forging a long-lasting relationship. The money will come and go. Strong relationships continue through the ups and downs.

Early on as a sales manager, I was surprised by how many customers we would lose when a sales rep retired, moved away, or was let go. I believed clients advertised with us because it worked well for them and brought in the results they needed. I eventually learned that when our top sales professionals left us, we would lose about 15–20 percent of their clients.

While results are important, they aren't the only factor in a buying relationship. I spoke with many clients who explained that while their advertisements had been effective for a while, when results dipped, they continued with us because of the relationship they had built with their rep.

Strong sales reps can make ad campaign results secondary. They do this by building genuine relationships forged by care, concern and trust.

If you are in sales and your turnover rates are high, take a few extra minutes with today's chapter. Know that you are the key driver for retention. You will need to adjust and improve if you hope to increase your success.

Last, inspire your co-workers, prospects and clients to remember that if you want a long-lasting relationship with someone (especially a team member or client), understand they cannot help but occasionally look elsewhere. Don't get upset with them. It's not their fault. The grass always looks greener on the other side. This is especially true in business, where there will always be competition. Don't be complacent. Expect your competitors

Show how your prospects can rely on you.

to come knocking. Simply keep the grass watered so your clients don't feel compelled to go explore.

If only a few people read this book, if only a few begin to live their lives with an attitude of gratitude, then the time spent working on it will have been worthwhile for me. My gratitude has been a source of tremendous inspiration in my life and helped create my passion for success. I hope yours does the same for you.

SLOW SPEED BUMP

Spend a few minutes reflecting on these questions, then add your thoughts to your notes.

- What are you grateful for?
- Who should you share your gratitude with today?

Make sure that nobody pays back wrong for wrong, but always strive to do what is good for each other and for everyone else. Rejoice always, pray continually, give thanks in all circumstances; for this is God's will for you in Christ Jesus.

1 Thessalonians 5:15–18

Day Sixteen
Eat Your Frog

THERE IS AN OLD SAYING that if the first thing you do each morning is eat a live frog, you will have the satisfaction of knowing you are done with the worst thing you must do all day.

Speaker and author Brian Tracy uses eating a frog as a metaphor for tackling your most challenging task. His best-selling book *Eat that Frog!* also emphasizes that getting daunting tasks done first can have the greatest impact on your life.

I always enjoyed sharing excerpts from Tracy's book in Clipper training sessions. It applies to your roadmap too because he also said:

> Successful people are where they are today because of their habits.

It wasn't an accident that I began asking you to build new daily habits even in the introduction of this book. Remember, to "get the good ones?"

I hope you see how these daily habits and your time reflecting on each day's Speed Bumps are moving you toward the success you have been striving for.

Today, I will cover the ways you can foster a strong habit of making the best use of your time. Personally, I would rather not have to eat a live frog if I can help it.

There are two fundamental keys to making the best use of your time.

- Understanding yourself and how your internal clock works.
- Understanding others and their internal clocks.

First, you must understand how you respond naturally to external demands. When I started in sales, my wife and I were newlyweds with two young children. When I moved into sales management, our kids were at ages that involved lots of extra-curricular activities that demanded more time and attention.

I could have easily fallen into the habit of procrastination, especially since it was difficult to accomplish everything on my plate. But, once you allow yourself to procrastinate in one thing, it becomes easier to do the same with almost everything else. Understanding yourself doesn't mean you're excusing your bad habits. It's simply the first step toward developing the good habits you need to be successful.

I am a morning person, which I mention only to illustrate the first area you can tackle. Most individuals are either night owls or morning people. It was crucial to make myself productive early in the day, as I would seldom have the energy for it after the kids went to bed. In the early morning before they woke up, though? I could get quite a bit done. The key was to figure out the tasks I could accomplish during this time and to do them. This freed me up for activities later in the day that required other individuals or could be done only at certain times. By using my time more effectively this way, it allowed me to be more productive.

It's not just about understanding when you're the most productive, though. Other people you need to connect with have their own internal clocks, too. I might have been a morning person, but many of my prospects, clients and even co-workers were not.

Early on at Clipper, I learned the importance of business owner availability. You can insert any stakeholder or relationship into this phrase, but the point is, you need to align your tasks that require collaboration or direct communication properly with the business owner's availability. To be successful, I needed to align my internal clock with those of others—they rarely worked according to mine.

Got that? To be successful, you need to understand both your internal clock and the clocks of others. You also need to understand its impact on your life, both personally and professionally.

Now let's build a strategy for making the best use of your time. There are four aspects of time you can work with to build daily habits that will allow you to be more productive.

- Time of day
- Time of year
- Time of events
- Time that is wasted

Start by building a plan to make good use of your most productive time of day. As I mentioned earlier, I am a morning person. I would welcome a sales presentation each day at

7:30 a.m. What a great way for me to start a productive day! The only problem was, not many business owners liked me knocking on their door that early. I spent a lot of my time selling to small retail stores, restaurants and home improvement contractors. Most retailers typically opened for business around 10:00 a.m. Restaurant owners often wouldn't want to see me during lunch or dinner hours. Contractors spent much of their day in the field. Sound like it's complicated to get any work done? Not really.

You just have to want to find a solution and then execute it. Whenever a client told me, "Come back on Thursday morning," I would joke with them, "Hey, I'm a morning person. What is 'morning' for you? How early would you like me here?" Naturally, most said somewhere around 10:00 a.m. But not always. Some said, "Hey, I'm here early as well. Want to stop in around 8:00 a.m.?" And I would say, "Absolutely! How about you start the coffee, and I'll bring the doughnuts?"

If you are a morning person and you can make a sale at 8:00 a.m., why would you ever wait to see that client until 10:00 a.m.? There are plenty of other clients you can't see until then. I would always see individuals who were fellow morning people early, thereby freeing up my most demanded time slots for others. Selling to small business owners gave me a productive window of about five hours a day. To be successful, I needed to stretch that window to eight hours a day. Often, accomplishing that was just a function of asking questions.

The largest and most important category for me to pursue when I was selling Clipper ads was the restaurants, since consumers love to eat out. They love to try new places, especially if they have a coupon to save money. Guess which clients offered me the smallest window of business owner availability? Yes, the restaurant owners! Most were small mom-and-pop places—busy owners with crazy hours. They didn't want to see me during lunch or dinner and would normally tell me to come in the midafternoon, between those two busy times. Sounds fine, right?

The problem was, these businesses skipped the most appointments with me. Once their lunch rush quieted down, they needed to leave the restaurant, if possible, to take care of personal errands before the dinner rush. They rarely worried about me showing up at 2:30, thinking they could sneak out after lunch ended around 2:00, which wasn't good for me! I learned to explain that unfortunately 2:30 wouldn't work for me, but I could see them at 1:30. No worries, I would tell them. If they were still busy, I would be glad to wait or stop back another time if that worked better. I knew I needed to get in front of them before they could escape for the afternoon.

Whatever stakeholder you need to meet with, examine their daily schedules and routines, then look for ways to fill your day productively.

The second aspect of time you can manage to your benefit, the time of year, is the easiest to accomplish, as long as your goal is to be as productive as possible.

I realized after my first two summers selling Clipper that New Jersey business owners were nowhere to be found during the week of the Fourth of July. Whether they were taking advantage of their spouses being on holiday or their business just happened to be slower, they would all head to the Jersey shore that week. There was no way to fill a slate of appointments during that time, so I simply learned to take my summer vacation the same week. I might as well enjoy myself instead of getting frustrated on those long, hot and humid summer days. I knew I would have to accomplish more than usual the week before the Fourth and set up a lot of appointments for when I returned.

As a sales manager, though, I was frustrated by how many sales reps refused to do the same. I would remind them every spring to book their summer vacation time effectively. Then, I would watch them have a slow week at the end of June, get nothing worthwhile done over the week of the Fourth, and finally head off for their vacations in mid-July. Their sales and income would always suffer.

Summer in New Jersey is just one example of understanding your sales year. Every industry has its seasons, conventions and busy periods. The key is to understand how the calendar impacts your success and then to plan accordingly.

Which leads us squarely into the time of events. Every life has events that take time and wreak havoc with schedules, whether school events, weddings, family get-togethers, or extended vacations. Forming the habit of looking ahead and anticipating these events can make all the difference and help you excel, despite the extra pressure they may put on your productivity.

By now, I think you understand the importance of having a strategy for how to use your time effectively and how you can develop one. To illustrate how events can affect your time management, I want to discuss one that many overlook: a deadline.

In sales, we all deal with deadlines. Every sales professional I ask seems to agree on one fact. They close more sales at or near deadlines than at any other time. I could spend an entire book exploring why. Is it the urgency a client feels as a deadline approaches? Does that urgency change the way the salesperson performs?

In truth, the reasons don't really matter. What matters is that it is often a fact. And as a salesperson, if I can make more sales near my deadlines, wouldn't it behoove me to spend all my time then on sales activities?

For most sales organizations, there are sales activities and other activities. We all have weekly tasks to accomplish that don't necessarily move a sale along. One big example at Clipper was the artwork. While I have talked about selling campaigns to new clients, understand that if we didn't produce a high-quality ad, an ad that looked great and brought strong results, we would lose that client.

Developing an ad meant combining several key elements. I needed to select the right photo to tell a story. I needed an attention-grabbing headline. I needed a call to action that brought customer traffic. Finding these ingredients took time, especially for a newer client—time after the sale itself, that wasn't directly part of moving that sale along, but rather part of fulfilling the sale itself.

We had a deadline for turning the ad's creative elements over to our artists, which ran concurrently with our space reservation deadlines. As a newer salesperson at Clipper, it was easy for me to procrastinate and not spend the necessary time on art early in a sales cycle. Often, I would get around to it only when the deadline was fast approaching, and it took me more time to develop the ad because I had to remember what I had discussed with my client back when they signed with me.

That meant spending a lot of effort on art right before the deadline, which took away from time I could spend selling more ads. At the deadline, when I could sell more new ads, I didn't have enough time to sell them. To be successful, I needed to start completing the art and other non-sales activities well before my sales deadlines so I could take advantage of one of my biggest sales events: my next mailing deadline.

There was an added benefit of getting the artwork done earlier in that the art department had more time to work with me, so the results weren't rushed and we ultimately created a better ad.

Finally, let's spend a minute exploring time that is wasted. I shared my concept of assumed appointments earlier and how they helped me be more productive in setting appointments. They were a very effective use of my time. I have spent far too many hours as a passenger in a sales rep's car, staring out a front windshield, driving all day, and then speaking with prospects for what seemed like mere minutes. I have never been the most patient of people. If I am spending a day riding with someone, hoping to help them make sales, then we darn well need to talk with more clients.

One of the main reasons I developed assumed appointments was to eliminate as much "windshield time" as possible. If I have an appointment in one town this morning, shouldn't I try to meet any other prospects nearby? Shouldn't I do this before venturing back behind that windshield again?

Most people simply waste too much time every day. You and your coworker may work the same number of hours, but the person who uses their time most effectively is always going to be more productive.

I know when I was in sales, when my workday started, look out and don't get in my way. When lunchtime arrived, it was drive-thru fast-food, so I didn't waste time.

Spend time making phone calls one day a week or at a certain time every day? No way. I started each day with a list of ten calls I needed or wanted to make. I never set aside time for them. I just made them when I had the time. If I stopped in to see a hair salon owner and they asked me to wait ten minutes while they finished with a customer, I would say, "Sure, no problem. If you don't mind, I'll wait outside in my car. I have a call to make."

Today, you need to develop the habit of having your most valuable asset—your time—working effectively for you. We all have the same amount of time in our day. Some just use it more wisely than others.

Why do so many struggle with procrastination? I think it's because they don't take it seriously. They're not connecting how procrastination is affecting their lives and success.

Many see procrastination as a joke more than anything more.

- "I do my work at the same time each day. The last minute!" — source unknown
- "I love deadlines. I love the whooshing noise they make as they go by." — Douglas Adams

When you finally realize the joke is actually on you and you only have so much precious time, that's when you develop daily habits to stop procrastinating and make the most of your time. Then, you can manage yourself to the success you desire.

There's always a solution. Find it.

Whenever I begin managing a new team of people, I always explain that I will never ask them to work more hours than they already do. Most of us spend far too many hours at work. I may, however, ask them to become more productive with the time they already spend working.

When you have chosen a path that can lead you where you want to go, the last thing you need are roadblocks. Procrastination and wasting time are two such obstacles that must be avoided. Some people may set a new daily habit to invest a few more hours every week to reach their career goals. Hopefully, you are instead simply seeking ways to make the time you currently spend more effective.

SLOW SPEED BUMP   **Spend a few minutes** reflecting on these questions, then add your thoughts to your notes.

- What are your key hours for sales interaction? Are you doing non-productive tasks then?
- List two to three ways you can make more productive use of your time.
- Do you make more sales near your deadlines? What other tasks are needed for your deadline that you can complete earlier to allow more time for sales?
- Do you have a life event coming up? What changes or plans should you begin making now?

Day Seventeen
Definition of Insanity

CLIPPER ELIMINATED my VP of Sales position on May 31, 2020. If I still woke up every day and put on my Clipper dress shirt (yes, I wore them almost daily for many years), some would call that insane. And I would agree.

German physicist Albert Einstein is often mis-attributed with saying:

> The definition of insanity is doing the same thing over and over again, but expecting different results.

It took me a few weeks after I lost my job, but I soon realized I needed to approach things in a new way. I am far too young to retire, and I still have a lot to offer.

Most of us go to work every day motivated and eager to be successful. We have a job to do, and we spend our time doing it. Unfortunately, that leaves us unprepared when that employment is ripped away from us.

If you have recently lost your job or lay awake at nights concerned about losing it, then it's time for a reality check. As a baby boomer, I grew up thinking I needed to focus all my efforts on my day job. My loyalty and dedication were to my employer. After twenty-eight years with that focus, I awakened to a much different labor market than when I had started.

We all have those unique gifts I wrote about. Gifts that have made us successful and qualities that future employers need to see. The problem is that even the best resume (expensively produced with all the right keywords) will undoubtedly get lost somewhere on the internet.

After I lost my job, I have learned the hard way that in today's labor market, it's not what you know or even who you know. It's who knows you. The twenty-eight years I remained focused on my little world left few outside it knowing anything about me.

While one of my gifts is that I have always had an immense will to win, what I didn't prepare for was a way to showcase that gift to those outside of Clipper. I spent several months playing catch-up, but you shouldn't have to.

You just need to focus on building your personal brand. Continue to perform in your day job like it is on the line—that never changes. That is always job #1. But it only takes a few hours every week to prepare for a future win, and you owe it to yourself to do so.

Network with companies and individuals in your industry. One benefit of the pandemic of 2020 was the rise of virtual networks. People wanted to connect. Now they know how to do it virtually and they like it, which makes them eager to network with others.

You can find groups, communities and associations for every industry, niche and backyard. Get to know others and help them know you.

Build your online presence to increase your brand. Show yourself to be a thought leader in your industry. You have subject matter expertise, so show it. Engage with others. Get to know them as they get to know you. Help future teammates and even employers envision the passion and knowledge you could bring to their organization.

Opportunities that may be perfect for you will open up, and if others know you well enough to recognize a good fit, they will share those opportunities with you.

Assess your unique gifts. What traits have made you successful in the past? Those are the gifts you need to showcase in your networking and social media presence.

Are you a dynamic speaker? Learn how to communicate with video to show off that ability.

Are you a strong communicator with knowledge to share? Post articles and valuable content weekly on LinkedIn and elsewhere.

Are you a fun and engaging teammate at work? Comment on the posts of others and share your humor, style and voice.

Perform a reality check. What future job or role would you like to have? Align your new daily branding habits with a vision of where you hope to be. Determine what resources you need. Now is the time to read, learn and prepare. (Kudos to you for doing just that by reading this book.)

Not sure where to begin? Reach out for help. Trust me, it is there. You can successfully build your personal brand in just a few hours a week. Simply use your current social media time differently. Instead of socializing, use it for educating and connecting with people. Then, you can enjoy going to work every day motivated and eager for success. But understand you

Get to know others and help them know you.

have a new job to do as well, creating a strong network for your-self. Your very own side hustle is to build your personal brand. Get excited! Your future starts now.

One of my favorite motivational authors and speakers was Charlie "Tremendous" Jones. I heard him speak in the mid-'90s. For over fifty years, he had a simple yet powerful mission: to help people improve their lives through reading. He once said:

> You will be the same person in five years as you are today except for the people you meet and the books you read.

As I reinvented myself after Clipper, I thought often about that quote. I have been able to avoid insanity thanks to the many people I have connected with and my willingness and desire to keep learning. I realized that my new dream job was out there. My passion for many years has been helping others grow in their sales and leadership careers. My dream job is doing that every day for individuals and small companies across the country. I want to be one of the "people you meet" that Charlie talked about—those that can help change your life.

So, I outlined the book you are now reading. I offered sales and leadership insights on LinkedIn. (Feel free to connect with me there! I would love to hear from you and be of value in any way I can.)

Finally, my wife and I started a sales podcast. I have always wanted to work closer with Kelly. Our podcast was such a bless-ing to us during the time we produced it together. It was a fun and rewarding show.

You see, you can't do things as you always have and expect different results. Times change, technology changes, and society changes with every generation. The fundamentals and gifts that have made you successful are still relevant, but you need to be open to new ways to use them.

SLOW SPEED BUMP

Spend a few minutes reflecting on these questions, then add your thoughts to your notes.

- Where do you want to be in five years?
- Who should you meet? How can you get in front of them today?
- Are you spending enough time on your personal brand? If not, how much time will you commit to it moving forward?
- What new approaches or ideas have you been avoiding out of a fear of change?
- What changes should you be making to how you use your social media time?

See, I am doing a new thing! Now it springs up; do you not perceive it? I am making a way in the wilderness and streams in the wasteland.

Isaiah 43:19

Day Eighteen
It's Not About What Your Mom Thinks

So, THERE I WAS, getting back into my car. The engine was idling as I took a sip of my now watered-down, still-sugary Dunkin iced coffee. Overnight rain clouds were clearing, but the morning sun was not yet shining, as it was forecasted to do for the afternoon. I turned on 610-WIP, my favorite local sports talk radio station, peeked in my rearview mirror, and reversed out of my parking spot. I had just finished an early sales presentation and felt pretty darn good. I had spent about thirty minutes discussing the features and benefits of running a new ad in my upcoming Clipper mailing with today's prospect. They smiled when they should have. They asked all the right questions. They even laughed at my attempts at humor.

But something just felt off. I stopped reversing, pulled back into my spot, and put my car back in park. I turned down the radio and took another sip of coffee. A question nagged me. If the appointment had gone as well as I felt, why wasn't I filing a signed contract right then?

Too often, I had backed out of similar parking spots and headed to my next appointment feeling just as good—enjoying my radio show, thinking about the rest of the day or calling my wife to see how her morning was going. Later in the week, I would be left wondering why that prospect hadn't called back and why they were no longer answering my emails or calls. Even worse, they would sometimes be too busy to come out of their back office to speak with me when I casually stopped by. I had ignored that nagging question and simply enjoyed feeling positive after too many other meetings left me with no signature to file.

In sales, you constantly need to ask, why didn't they sign the contract? It doesn't help to back out of that parking spot and drive away feeling as if everything is perfect. In reality, it often isn't perfect, and there are improvements you need to make.

It was a hard lesson to learn, but an important one. After that, I would stop and take a few minutes in the car before leaving after each presentation. While it was still fresh in my mind, I needed to give myself constructive feedback. A sale had not been made. Why? What could I have done differently? If there are materials I could have shown but didn't, now is the time to write that down. Did I completely answer their objections? If not, how can I deal with them better on my next visit? Then, suddenly, I remember points I wish I had made in my presentation. Quickly, I jot them down. If I hadn't made the sale, where was the disconnect between my offer and their current needs? There was room for improvement. This simple, fundamental self-awareness made a huge impact on my sales.

I have worked with far too many salespeople who insist they did everything right. They nailed it! Well, I can assure you, if you left without a sale, you didn't nail it. You may have done well, but you should still analyze what you could have done better. The most successful salespeople leave even big sales thinking there was room for improvement. The best way to improve any of your skills is through feedback, both good and bad.

Feedback isn't listening to what your mom says about you. Trust me, if I believed what my mom says about me, I would never work a day in my life. Why would I need to? In her eyes, I am perfect in about every possible way. Good things will happen to me because they just should. I am that perfect.

There are two kinds of moms in this world.

A mom like mine can only see the good in me. She encourages me, believes in me. She has always had my back and allowed me to attack the world knowing she would always be there for me. No matter what. She filled me with confidence and encouragement. Whatever I did, it was a great idea. She helped fuel the ego that later would be so important to me when I was a growing salesperson.

There really is nothing like the love of a mother. But this kind of mom is not the person you can trust for honest feedback.

Even worse is the other type of mom, the one who consistently points out all your flaws, tells you you won't succeed, and discourages everything you try. I consider this far worse. It also shouldn't be where you go for honest feedback.

Kelly fondly recalls her mom as being in the middle, always positive and encouraging, always there for her, but not one to encourage unrealistically. Kelly hopes we are raising our children the same way. I do too, but I admit that, no matter how much we try, we will always err toward the positive, toward encouragement. I hope our children look for honest feedback from others. For feedback to be effective, it must be both positive and negative. We are not perfect people. We all have room to grow.

The first form of feedback to help make you successful has to start from within. You are the only one who completely understands all you do. You not only see your accomplishments but understand your intentions as well. To understand your strengths and weaknesses, you need a realistic view of yourself. When you welcome your weaknesses, you can learn how to improve them or find ways to work around them. Self-awareness is a critical factor for any successful person.

Just like Mom can't always see the full picture, neither, sometimes, can you. Therefore, you need to find people in your life willing to share feedback with you, which is the second type of feedback you need to grow. Mentors, managers and sometimes friends can all help here. The key is trust and respect. Look for feedback from people you admire and those you trust to have your best interests at heart—people who want to see you improve and succeed. Too often, we listen to feedback from those who aren't really interested in us improving.

I don't believe anyone genuinely likes hearing negative feedback. You don't have to like it to learn from it. I doubt I will ever enjoy hearing about things I struggle with. (Ask my wife, who, like a saint, has read and critiqued each page of this book so far.) My first instinct upon hearing negative feedback is usually to debate, deny or rebut it. Later, though, when I sit back and reflect, I begin to understand and then to learn. I have never been eager to receive it, but I have learned how important it has been in my growth. I wish I was more receptive to feedback when I was younger.

When those around us stop offering helpful feedback, it is often because of our reaction to what they offer. If you want information that will be instrumental to your growth, show those around you you're willing to positively receive their feedback. When someone has given you constructive criticism that helps you to improve, let them know the impact they have made on you.

Now, before you start to offer me some negative feedback—"Hey, how about you get back on track with sales training here?"—I do have a couple of tips that always helped me in sales. But first, I welcome your feedback on this book. I'd love it if you'd leave a review on your favorite book retail site. All input is welcome.

My first tip for you has to do with self-awareness and how it can affect your sales. Each of us has a distinct personality and traits that fit into one of several sales styles, with most reps fitting into a particular one.

To illustrate, consider those reps who are strong relationship builders. I have worked with many people who fit this profile. They are also probably my favorite type of people, as they are normally the nicest and most caring of individuals. They develop strong feelings for their clients and consider many of them to be friends. If you surveyed their client base, you would typically receive rave reviews. They often keep their clients longer and excel with renewals, while seeming to enjoy their careers more with the highest job satisfaction.

But relationship builders also have weaknesses. They often struggle if their sales cycles are fast-paced, spending too much time working with each client to the detriment of other job

Your clients are giving you feedback. Listen to it.

tasks. Unfortunately, they are also prone to wasting time with prospects, fostering relationships that never result in sales.

I have worked with many amazing reps who fit this profile, but the successful ones all had to find ways to work around the weaknesses that came with it. Those who struggled to find a solution worked far more hours than they may have liked.

I could easily fill an entire book explaining the different rep profiles and all the good and bad traits for each. But the goal here is just to make you aware of yours. Ask yourself what personality traits you have and honestly look for feedback on what your trusted resources consider your strengths and weaknesses to be.

Finally, let's spend a few minutes on sales feedback, which can be instrumental in helping you close more deals. It doesn't matter if you are selling ad space or computer software. Learning to get this sort of feedback during your presentation is crucial, since it will help you assess how engaged your prospect is with what you have to sell them.

If you haven't heard of the concept of a test close, it's not merely a sales or closing technique. A test close is simply feedback received well before a negative outcome. It is a way for you to see if someone is engaged with you. Are you connecting with them? Are you on the road to solving their problems? Are you on the same page?

A proper test close never makes the other person defensive. It gives them an easy out. I would much rather discover after a brief ten-minute conversation that we aren't moving toward a possible sale. I would rather learn this from a quick test close now than forty-five depressing minutes later. Performed early enough, a test close can offer the feedback that allows us to try a different approach or find a new way to engage.

Remember I mentioned earlier about how every business was unique and you needed to develop a different roadmap to get from point A to point B for each? Test closes are often the best way to learn when a new approach needs to be explored. Or it can simply save you valuable time.

One test close technique I wanted to share is what I liked to call "putting them to work." When I was selling Clipper, I always needed to know where else my prospects were already advertising. During a presentation, I wanted to compare their other ads alongside my magazine.

Of course, I should be properly prepared, bringing a few copies of those other ads with me. Although it would mean I could easily pull them out to compare, I preferred to ask them if they would do me a favor and get a copy of their recent ads. I would explain that I would love to see them and offer some ideas. Their willingness to take the time to get them could be an indicator to just how interested they were in my presentation.

If a business owner was engaged with my presentation and saw me as a valued consultant, they would welcome my input on their ads. They were more willing to "do the work" to go get them for me. The longer it took to retrieve them, the more excited I became—this gave me an idea of how invested they were in working with me.

If, instead, the business owner told me they weren't sure where to find an ad quickly, that didn't mean the presentation was a dud, but it did give me some important feedback: I still had a lot to accomplish. Did I need to try a different approach? Maybe. Either way, I had gained some useful information.

Another opportunity for a test close was a true favorite at Clipper, one I am sure can be copied in almost every type of sale. I would build exciting and beautiful ad campaigns for our clients with catchy headlines, cool photos, and a strong call to action. Many of my sales presentations progressed far enough that we would discuss what a client's ad might look like, asking for details about what they planned to offer, what photo they wanted to use, and securing a copy of their logo.

Here was another opportunity to see how engaged this prospect was. Were they interested in discussing the elements of an ad? If they were, that was a good sign. If they got up and went to look for photos or booted up their computer to show me a logo, that was a great sign. And if they claimed they weren't sure what they might show or offer? Then maybe it was time for another approach.

These are just a couple examples. Test closes like these enable you to receive immediate feedback about your presentation or call, which can provide valuable insight that can help you steer past an approaching dead end. Just like personal feedback can help you grow as a salesperson, immediate sales feedback like this can turn a failing presentation into a rewarding sale.

Constructive and honest feedback will be vital to your success in so many ways. Do not rely on your mom telling you how you are doing.

SLOW SPEED BUMP

Spend a few minutes reflecting on these questions, then add your thoughts to your notes.

- Perform an honest self-evaluation of where you are at as a salesperson. What resources should you be looking for that will help with the improvement you desire?

- What weaknesses do you have in your personality traits that may be affecting your sales? How can you strengthen them?

- How can you "put your customers to work" to gain feedback in how engaged they are with your presentation?

- What test closes should you be working into your calls, virtual meetings, and sales presentations? How can you introduce one subtly?

Day Nineteen
We All Need Passion

WHENEVER I NEEDED TO GET UP and get running, whenever I needed to get motivated, whenever I needed to prepare for a huge meeting, I loved listening to Rod Stewart singing his '80s hit song "Passion." In it, he sings about how a lot of people don't have passion. He was so right. Many people aren't passionate.

I found that thought motivating. It gave me a leg up on my competition. I had passion. I was motivated and running. If everybody had passion, it would be more difficult to stand out from my competition. For me, the right words with the right music just got me going.

Where does passion come from? I believe it starts with confidence. Confidence without fear. Listening to the right words with the right music helped me forget my fears and pumped up that confidence even when it seemed not to be there.

Are you searching for some passion? A passion to be more successful? Since you are reading this book, I will assume the answer is "yes." So, today, I will cover how you should have already started to build it. Let's see where the day takes you.

Looking for the right words and music? I can't help with that, but have fun. It is out there. Find it. Enjoy it. And please, *play it loud*, and play it often.

You likely know passion when you see it in others. Passionate people seem to exude confidence. They are usually smiling and enthusiastic. We typically engage with them because their passion creates an excitement that's contagious.

What is one of the first things you notice when someone is passionate about a given topic? A passionate person will ask a lot of questions to show they care about you. When you sense this passion and engage with them by answering their questions, you may truly open up and really share with them. It's common to share so much more when speaking with someone who is passionate than with someone who is not.

This is one reason why passionate salespeople can be so successful. They form deeper relationships and build rapport quicker than dispassionate people. For salespeople, this is a huge advantage.

While all my sales presentations were unique, they each followed a specific roadmap. The exact road may vary, but I could not reach my destination without spending ample time on the road I called the interview. That was where I built rapport and trust with a client and where I learned what they wanted, needed and could afford. It was where they showed me which route would be most likely to arrive at a sale today. The probing questions I asked were designed to learn about them and to build rapport and trust by showing them I cared and wanted to understand their likes and dislikes. Those objectives were more important than my features and benefits. This phase of the sales interview can be crucial to your success.

When I started with Clipper, we had a major competitor to contend with. While our advertising product was a beautiful, full-color magazine, this competitor produced an envelope full of coupons and ads. The format of our products may have differed, but we were very much alike. We both offered money-saving ads and offers directly mailed into people's homes, and we both offered business owners a way to get their message out to our readers, hopefully driving traffic and sales to them.

Most Clipper reps believed we had a better product and better value. Our challenge was to demonstrate that to a current envelope advertiser—especially when we were often more expensive. My goal in these appointments was to passionately engage with a client, building trust and getting them to open up and share what they liked and disliked about their envelope ads.

Many were pleased with their ads and enjoyed good results from them. In that case, I needed to applaud what they had accomplished and show our magazine was remarkably similar. Then I could illustrate how we might deliver even stronger results.

If, on the other hand, I learned during my interview that they were displeased with their envelope advertising, I needed to venture down a different road. I needed to illustrate right away the many differences between our products.

Remember Feel, Felt, Found from Day Twelve? I would show them I understand how they feel. Many current clients felt the same way. Here is what they found when they used our direct mail magazine.

In the end, it didn't really matter whether these business owners liked or disliked envelope advertising. What mattered was that I knew how they felt before I showed them the features and benefits of my product.

Passionately engaging with a client caused them to open up and share more. What they told me helped me choose the road to a solution they could picture helping them.

The more passion someone sees in you, the more they open up and engage. You can't fake passion. You truly need to care. I left many appointments without a sale because I realized I didn't have a solution for their problem. I never faked passion. I *had* passion. It came from the confidence that I could solve most of my clients' advertising needs and I wasn't afraid to present my solutions.

Looking to build on your passion? Well, let's take that first test together. Passion comes from confidence. Confidence comes from knowledge. Knowledge comes from learning every day.

As you've been reading this book, I've been sharing habits to build your confidence. Are you practicing them daily?

I challenged you early on to avoid taking shortcuts. A shortcut would be reading this book and not doing the exercises or without selecting a few daily habits to practice. Or worse yet, taking the insane approach of reading this book, continuing to do things the way you always have, and expecting different results. Remember, I asked you to do all that was expected of you and just a little bit more.

Do you already have all the confidence you need? Good. Carry on and use that passion.

Still trying to develop more passion? Still looking for a few cool tips or best practices? Well, no worries. Just like with a sales presentation, you can take that feedback and adjust your course.

1. Have you begun adopting some of the key habits you hopefully have been building as you have read this book?

2. Do you understand your unique gifts? Are you using the traits that have made you successful in the past in every encounter, every time? If you are, you're going to enjoy selling with a passion that keeps you smiling and enthusiastic about what you do.

3. Are you taking steps daily to have luck on your side? Remember, your road to greatness is a journey! By now, you have hopefully crafted, refined and continually practiced your thirty-second commercial. When you meet someone now, are you ready and confident to put on a show!

4. Have you become a better listener? Are you paying more attention to your words and how they impact others? I hope so! When you slow down, it gives you time to consider more thoughtful replies. Becoming an attentive listener will help you read clients and situations better than ever before.

5. Are you performing at your best even when no one is watching, every day? Stop making excuses. Be a problem solver.

6. Are you trying to embrace change? Have you accepted that change is happening and success will come when you begin to adjust? I hope you have added a few new daily habits that you had previously resisted. By

Knowledge leads to confidence, which creates passion.

now, you should be gaining more confidence in these new approaches.

7. Have you decided each day how you can be of value to your prospects and customers? Spent time bringing them value? Realized you get paid for the value you bring, not merely for your time? Is this helping you to build trust? And remember, keep it simple, stupid.

8. Has preparation become part of your daily habits? Sales can be explained very easily: sell to new clients, while keeping your old clients. You don't have to be perfect. You just need to prepare for the quality touches, having the right approach and the right materials at the right time.

9. Have you found yourself sharing in the pain of your clients? Are you working to align with them better? Give them room to be creative.

10. Have you been eating a live frog each morning? Okay, probably not. I get it! But have you found ways to manage your time better? Reduce wasted time, not only so you can work hard, but play hard too.

11. Have you stopped doing the same things every day when they aren't working, expecting them suddenly to yield different results? Instead, begin to practice self-reflection and look for honest feedback to help you grow.

If you have decided to change some of your daily habits, if you agree that it is just as easy to develop good habits as bad ones, if you are building up the confidence to start feeling more passion... the final two chapters should excite you. If you aren't feeling that excitement today, there is at least a little good news: I am not asking you to take any notes today.

Day Twenty
At 212 Degrees, Water Boils

NOW THAT YOU HAVE FOUND your passion, it's time to take control of your success. I have managed many people who had all the right ingredients to be successful, everything they needed, but who struggled with understanding how to guide their conversations. They struggled to seize the opportunity.

Are you ready to commit yourself? You must be to take control of your success. Need a little more incentive? Let me tell you about the extra little degree that is the difference between good and great.

One of my all-time favorite books is *212° The Extra Degree* by Sam Parker and Mac Anderson. This one short excerpt means so much to me:

> At 211 degrees, water is hot. At 212 degrees, it boils. And with boiling water, comes steam. And steam can power a locomotive. Raising the temperature of water by one extra degree means the difference between something that is simply very hot and something that generates enough force to power a machine.

If you ever struggle to find commitment or to push yourself that extra little degree, I encourage you to read *212° The Extra Degree*.

Day Twenty is all about being committed to taking the control you need. If you have done all the little things and built good habits; if your supervisor, spouse or friends have noticed a little difference in you; if you are seeing the signs of increased sales; or gain the confidence to apply for that upcoming promotion or new role... then all that is left may be to seize control. Let's discuss how.

Which daily habits on the list you've put together over the first nineteen chapters are things you have never done before? Can you commit to doing something new? Are you ready to guide your conversations skillfully?

In any relationship or sales endeavor, there will come a time for someone to take control and put themselves in the driver's seat to move a sale along.

As Ben Affleck said when playing senior broker Jim Young in the movie *Boiler Room*:

> And there is no such thing as a no sales call. A sale is made on every call you make. Either you sell the client some stock or he sells you on a reason he can't. Either way a sale is made. The only question is who is gonna close? You or him? Now be relentless, that's it, I'm done.

Today, will you be in the driver's seat or will your prospect? You have a solution that can help them, but who will be in control? Will you be able to demonstrate your value? It may now all come down to this. Who will be taking control of your success?

There was a seemingly trivial technique I would teach all new sales reps at Clipper. It was a small detail, but it had a big impact on who would control their sales presentation. Many of the magazines we used as samples were well over forty-eight pages, with dozens of advertisements. When we met with a prospect, we normally had several ads we wanted to emphasize to them—ads important to the story we wanted to tell them.

A newer salesperson would routinely allow the prospect to take hold of the magazine during their meeting. That meant they had lost control of which ads were being looked at. There was no way to control which page the prospect was drawn to or what questions they asked.

The newer salesperson needed to learn the importance of keeping the magazine in their hands, highlighting the pages they wanted to talk about and the key messages they wanted to cover. It seems like a simple concept, but there could be a huge difference in results based simply on who controlled the magazine.

A good salesperson also learned that while you sometimes had to allow a prospect to hold the magazine, you should never panic. Instead, you simply stopped talking. You waited for them to page through and look on their own.

When someone focuses on something as they flip through the pages, they won't be listening to most of what you say. Therefore, you should say nothing. Hold your presentation until you can retake control and have the magazine again. It doesn't matter what product or service you are selling. Take a close look at your presentation and ask yourself at what key moments you need to be in total control and command the prospect's complete attention. Now, work on the things you can do to keep that control.

Put yourself in the driver's seat to move a sale along.

Make yourself at home. This may seem like another small detail. But I can't emphasize enough how important it is. Making yourself at home comes into play in a variety of different ways. Wouldn't having your prospect meet you at your favorite restaurant give you an extra level of comfort? Now, imagine selling ads door-to-door or even selling to consumers and standing outside the front door of someone's home. How successful will you be standing in the doorway?

Whenever I had an appointment with a business, their first choice for where to meet would normally be their front counter. Here, they were in control. They could keep an eye on their business and even interrupt me to handle a customer, if needed. They would give me some attention, but never all of it. And they preferred it that way. They were in control.

My goal before any appointment would be to get them somewhere else. I would ask if we could sit at a table in the back. If their business was in a strip center or had a restaurant nearby, could I buy them a cup of coffee next door? I would explain I had brought several great ads to show them, and it might be helpful to do so in a more relaxed setting. Sometimes this worked, sometimes it didn't. But it never worked if I didn't ask.

This simple detail—making myself at home, more in my comfort zone than theirs—would be crucial in capturing their undivided attention. Nothing is worse than being on a roll with a solid presentation and having it interrupted by a customer or other distraction. There I am, working my way up to a climactic finish, about to show them how I could solve their problems, about to show them how I could save them money, only for them to say, "Hold on a sec." The momentum is gone. A huge sale is about to go down the drain. Even worse, they might come back after several minutes proclaiming we should reschedule.

If that happens, good luck getting back in front of them! That's worse than not having a presentation at all: the prospect listened for a while and now thinks they know all about the product... but I never got to the good part. I never gave them the solution they needed.

Unfortunately, taking control is one situation where the nice guy finishes last every time. People seldom surrender control easily. So, how do you make yourself at home? How do you take control? You seize it!

I wrote earlier about all those quality touches: about planning and preparation, and how all those things work together to present an opportunity to take control. Well, today I want to share with you my favorite way to prepare to guide your conversations. This is my "Cool Hat Story." It may not be as cool a story as I like to think, but it's a good one to leave you with, since you can't always force control when the timing isn't right.

Remember I mentioned earlier about how you needed to have luck on your side? You did this by creating opportunities for luck to work for you.

I created opportunities for luck to work for me as I was working on the streets, going door-to-door each day. I would picture myself as being relaxed walking around with my baseball cap on backward, looking and feeling pretty cool—just a salesperson feeling no pressure and under no sense of urgency. Confident, cocky and easy-going.

From this perspective, I was simply running around town talking with business owners, having a great time showing them how passionate I was about our magazine. I was just a happy-go-lucky publicist with no pending deadlines or pressure to make a sale. Much of each day was spent like this, doing my public relations work while I waited. Waited for what? For that quality touch when the business owner looked at cool Tom and opened the door for him to take control.

When they opened it, I would pounce! (In a helpful well-meaning way, of course.) The opportunity may have been a question about buying, or they may have mentioned an upcoming promotion they needed to market. They may have asked when my next magazine would be mailed, or they may just ask, "How much is that again?"

There were many ways for them to open the door. And I would be ready. I would simply imagine myself adjusting my cap, turning it facing forward. I was now wearing my professional sales hat. They had opened the door, and it was now time for me to make myself at home and take control.

If I approached a business owner trying to pressure the sale to move along every time, they wouldn't want to speak with me. The door might never be opened. But they opened the door to cool hat Tom because of his patience and efforts to engage and stand out.

At 211 degrees, water is very hot. At 212 degrees, it boils. I hope you have the commitment you need for the success you are looking for, and that you now see you may just need to turn up the heat that one extra degree to power yourself to move mountains. Work ethic, integrity and passion are all great. But to Be the Steak you were meant to be, you must take control.

When you pass through the waters, I will be with you; and when you pass through the rivers, they will not sweep over you. When you walk through the fire, you will not be burned; the flames will not set you ablaze.

Isaiah 43:2

Day Twenty-One
Honda or Tesla

M Y WIFE KELLY AND I started dating in 1984, and I was with her that summer day when her stepfather accompanied her while she bought her first car. It was glorious. A 1982 Honda Accord hatchback. What made it glorious? That amazing hatchback. It easily stored and kept accessible all the softball equipment we needed for our team's games. Okay, so maybe it was a little more glorious for me, but Kelly loved her first car too. I think we all have a special place in our hearts for our first car.

I fondly recall those early years of our dating—our first movie, our first apartment, the excitement of planning our wedding... They all pale in comparison to reminiscing about that first car. Okay, I may be exaggerating slightly—but it was a great car.

Kelly and I spent the rest of the '80s and '90s driving several vehicles, many of which were hand-me-downs that required numerous trips to the service station.

By 2000, things were going well for us and we gladly found our way back to Honda. We bought Kelly her first utility vehicle, the Honda CR-V. Our children were ten and twelve years old, ages with a lot of activities and things to transport.

In 2003, we traded that car in for our first minivan, the Honda Odyssey. We needed even more room. The kids were growing, they had even more activities, and we had our first vacation home to travel to. The entire family fell in love with skiing, and the minivan made the short drives from southern New Jersey to our place in the Pocono mountains of Pennsylvania much more enjoyable.

By 2009, the kids didn't find time with Mom and Dad exciting anymore. Kelly and I still wanted more room, but not quite as much as a minivan. We purchased another—you guessed it— Honda. This time, we went for the next generation of the CR-V.

By 2013, both Kelly and I were driving Hondas. While Kelly was comfortable in her sporty new Accord, I went to the dealership as the CR-V lease expired, expecting not to lease another Honda. The long hours on the road, as well as my age, were playing havoc with my lower back. It didn't seem like a larger, more comfortable Honda was available. But then I found the Honda Crosstour. I quickly fell in love. To this day, that car is without question the most comfortable ride I have ever had. I have leased Fords, Cadillacs and a Subaru, but none were as good to my body as that Crosstour.

Luckily for my back, my seemingly endless road trips were in fact nearing an end by 2017. Thanks to video meetings, I now spent most of my time working from home. Kelly and I were downsizing, and we decided to have only one car payment. And the one car we owned at this point was...? That's right: a Honda. This time, a Honda Civic. It was perfect for us. Over thirty-five years of dating and marriage, we have owned seven Hondas; between 2000 and 2019, we always had at least one parked in our driveway. It's safe to say we believe in Honda vehicles.

If someone asked us for a testimonial, we would be happy to provide it. I hope you have enjoyed this brief story—a brief glimpse into the history of Bloomer automobiles. I have spent time sharing it because I believe storytelling is one of the most important things you can do. It is incredibly powerful in sales. Whether you are walking into your local bakery, venturing into your neighborhood store, or buying a family car, storytelling helps move a sale along.

I worked from home the last few years I was with Clipper, although I was still involved in many of our training programs and conducted several sales meetings. Often, I would include a segment on "what my sales life would be like" when my Clipper days ended. I enjoyed this segment. I would explain that I had absolutely no worries about my sales future.

To be successful, you must first believe in yourself. You must also believe in your product. And what better product for me to sell successfully than Hondas? If a newlywed couple walks into the showroom, I've got a story for them. When a family of four with young children stops by, I've got their story too. The family of six, with older children and travel plans? I've got that one. The retired couple that shares back pain stories? I've *so* got that one. I would have all the confidence needed to make a great living selling Hondas. I might not even need my old Rod Stewart cassettes… For me, passion comes from confidence.

Of course, in almost every training session, there would be that one smart-alecky character who couldn't wait to ask

Be a passionate storyteller to connect with your prospects.

a question or two. "Tom, wouldn't you be able to earn more money selling a car like a Tesla? What if the Honda dealership near you isn't hiring?"

Luckily, these were just the two questions I was hoping to hear. This is where I would hammer home the central message of this training session. By this time, Clipper had diversified into much more than just a direct mail magazine. We offered a variety of postcards and inserts, built webpages and loyalty apps for small business owners, and had other digital offerings. In truth, the pages in our magazine were no longer our top-performing product. But many of our veteran salespeople and sales leaders still believed more in the product they had stood behind and sold effectively for so long. Their best stories and testimonials were about our magazine. They were comfortable with it and believed in it.

My message was that although I would be an amazing salesperson for a Honda dealership, I had no doubt I could also do well selling a Tesla. Now I told them, I had never driven a Tesla. All I knew about them was that I had heard they were better for the environment, but they were also more expensive than any car I'd ever owned. If my local Honda dealer isn't hiring and I am given a job opportunity with Tesla... Well, I'll use the next twenty-one days to manage myself into being an amazing seller of Tesla vehicles.

I hope this chapter has illustrated for you one of my favorite parts of sales: being a passionate storyteller. Where does that passionate story come from? Use the habits you've been developing to reflect on the experience you've had with your product. Which stories would resonate most with the people you're likely to meet?

Going back to my Tesla tale, if I have twenty-one days to develop some stories for my new job, it means I need to speak with people who have driven a Tesla. I need to learn its features and benefits. I already believe in myself, but I need to foster a belief in this new product too. If I can't find that belief in the next three weeks, I should find somewhere else to work. Not because I can't be a successful salesperson, but because I can't successfully sell this product.

When a newlywed couple walks into the Tesla showroom, I need a story for them. When a family of four with young children walks in, I need their story too. The family of six, with older children and travel plans? I need that. The retired couple who shares their back pain stories? I have to have one for them too.

Once I have those stories, look out: I will be driving to work, singing my favorite songs, ready to help everyone that enters the showroom today.

You don't need a better manager. You don't need a better product. You don't need a better life. You hold the key to success in your own hands. You always have.

So, wake up tomorrow and manage your way to success.

> "'If you can?'" said Jesus. "Everything is possible for one who believes."
>
> Mark 9:23

Day Twenty-Two
The Journey Continues

WHILE YOUR JOURNEY CONTINUES, the road to success is still under construction. Over the last twenty-one days, you've left the scenic route behind and paved your way while learning to stretch yourself.

I hope you are more motivated and hungry for success than when you started. You should now see your way clear of the many roadblocks and dead ends that plagued you in the past. There will still be some detours, foggy mornings, and long days as you navigate onward.

Keep running!

You will still be facing daily objections. Prospects will still tell you, "I am happy with my current provider," "I have no budget left," "Your product is too expensive," and "I am just not interested." There will be phone calls that aren't returned and emails that remain unopened. You will still encounter negative influences in your life. There will be stress and difficult deadlines and quotas.

Simply reading this book won't change anything. You need to put what you've learned into practice daily. When you're feeling discouraged, review your notes. Do you need to make any changes or updates to your roadmap?

The journey you began doesn't have a finish line. Your attitude, desire and work ethic are now even more important.

You've decided where you want to be. Stay committed to getting there. In Day Nineteen, I provided a series of questions for you to answer. Review them weekly. They will remind you of the many little habits that will help you succeed.

I also recommend re-reading this book periodically so you can adjust your notes as your sales journey evolves. The road block you began overcoming last week as a result of putting what you've learned into practice will no longer be an issue for you six months from now. What new road block will you want to tackle then?

They say it takes as little as twenty-one days to turn a new habit into a regular practice. You are on the right path. Keep your eyes on the road you are now following and establish firm guardrails for your new practices.

A career in sales can be extremely rewarding and enjoyable. When you are selling the right way and for the right reasons, it can be a career to be proud of. You started three weeks ago with a desire to achieve the success you've been striving for. As you approach that success, keep in mind something author and sales coach Jeffrey Gitomer taught me many years ago in his *Little Red Book of Selling*.

If you're not on fire, you will lose to someone who is.

I hope you have enjoyed reading *Teach Me Sales,* and you now realize that fire, that passion, is already inside you...

Keep it stoked every day to achieve the success you were born for!

— Tom Bloomer

Thank you for reading *Teach Me Sales*. If you've enjoyed reading this book, please leave a review on your favorite review site. It helps me reach more readers who may benefit from the information provided here.

Acknowledgments

O N DAY FIFTEEN, I wrote about the importance of developing an attitude of gratitude. I think it's an essential part to living a satisfying life. With all the success you may strive for along the way, none of it would be possible completely on your own.

In that chapter, I told you about my mom, Sharon, and how instrumental she was to building my confidence because she always had my back. I can never properly express how grateful I am for her love.

My wife, Kelly, has always been my biggest supporter. She has seen me at my weakest moments and has always been encouraging. No matter what goal I've stretched for, she's been there for me, whatever the outcome, and I'll be forever grateful for that.

When I became a father, my life completely changed. I suddenly cried during emotional movies. I felt more fear than I had ever imagined. I learned what it is to love someone more than yourself. God has blessed Kelly and me with the most amazing children. Ryan and Kayla give us something to live for and look forward to every day. As young parents, we have been able to grow up with our kids, not only as parents but also as friends. We have been so fortunate, and we are so thankful.

Along our journey, Kelly and I have had the best of family. My father, Tom, and his wife, Ruth. My stepfather, Rich, who raised me and taught me so much, and his wife, Gladys. Kelly's mom, Judy, someone I will always consider one of my best friends, and my father-in-law, Monty. My little brother Richard, who will always have a special place in my heart and has always been there for me, and Ron Stover, a long-time family friend who has always been so supportive to me and my children. Finally, I would truly not be where I am today without the love, friendship and guidance of my grandparents, Howard and Laura Samuels.

I got my start in the education business and achieved early success and growth thanks to being given a unique opportunity seldom given to someone as young and inexperienced as I was. This opportunity allowed me to learn a great deal and helped pave the way for future successes. I owe amazing gratitude to Karen Manin and Harry Commisso for that chance.

I have hopefully already expressed the awesome gift given to me in being part of Clipper Magazine. It truly was a family. It will always be the best years of my career. Steve Zuckerman, Bob Zuckerman, Ian Ruzow, and Rob Liss created that family. They gave me just enough rope and encouraged me to grow and find my way. They offered a life for my family I probably would never have been able to provide without them. I will forever appreciate what they did for us.

To Steve Hauber, who became CEO of Clipper when the original founders retired, thanks for your patience and efforts to carry on what had been started. Thanks for still being in my corner today.

Team Jersey! You know who you are. I will forever be thankful for all of you. We spent so many amazing times together.

My sincere thanks to Barry Cohen of AdLab Media, who has been working tirelessly to help me connect and reach so many of you via our sales podcast.

To the team at Emerald Lake Books... Tara Alemany and Mark Gerber are the reason you have found and are enjoying this book. Their expertise and guidance have enabled me to complete a project that otherwise would still be only a dream.

As I have mentioned before, I know in my heart this dream has been a gift from God—a gift I might very well have missed out on if it weren't for Kelly and I discovering Peak City Church in Apex, North Carolina. God led us to Peak City and made a home there for us. Special thanks to our pastor, Nate Marriner, our weekly small group, and everyone there who impacts our hearts everyday.

Finally, to my LinkedIn network and Facebook sales community, your connections, engagement and messages have meant so much during a difficult transition in my career. Thanks for always being there.

Author's Note

YOU MAY REMEMBER from the Introduction that I have found instruction and encouragement in the Bible throughout my career. And I'd like to share a few of my favorite passages with you, for those who might benefit from it.

During the many times I struggled as a young salesman, I took courage from Isaiah 41:10.

> So do not fear, for I am with you; do not be dismayed, for I am your God. I will strengthen you and help you; I will uphold you with my righteous right hand.

Communication and encouragement have been vital for my growth, as taught to me by 1 Thessalonians 5:11.

> Therefore encourage one another and build each other up, just as in fact you are doing.

As I learned to be an "Ah, there you are" type of person, Romans 12:3 put things into perspective for me.

> For by the grace given to me I say to every one of you: Do not think of yourself more highly than you ought, but rather think of yourself with sober judgment, in accordance with the faith God has distributed to each of you.

I became more mindful of the influence of others on me and how my words impact other people, thanks to James 1:19–20.

> My dear brothers and sisters, take note of this: Everyone should be quick to listen, slow to speak and slow to become angry, because human anger does not produce the righteousness that God desires.

Doing all the little things in life often results in significant rewards, just like the mustard seed we read about in Matthew 13:32.

> Though it is the smallest of all seeds, yet when it grows, it is the largest of garden plants and becomes a tree, so that the birds come and perch in its branches.

I have learned to share my plans with the Lord and ask for his guidance, thanks to Proverbs 16:3 and 16:9.

> Commit to the Lord whatever you do, and he will establish your plans. In their hearts humans plan their course, but the Lord establishes their steps.

All that I have and all that I do are thanks to the Lord, as per Colossians 3:17.

> And whatever you do, whether in word or deed, do it all in the name of the Lord Jesus, giving thanks to God the Father through him.

As I look back on my life, I see how important planning and preparation have been, even as we're told in John 9:4 and Proverbs 21:5, respectively.

> As long as it is day, we must do the works of him who sent me. Night is coming, when no one can work.
> The plans of the diligent lead to profit as surely as haste leads to poverty.

We must always consider feedback regarding our actions, motives and desires according to Lamentations 3:40.

> Let's examine our ways and test them, and let us return to the Lord.

I have learned from 1 Corinthains 10:13 that God never gives me more than I can handle.

> No temptation has overtaken you except what is common to mankind. And God is faithful; he will not let you be tempted beyond what you can bear. But when you are tempted, he will also provide a way out so that you can endure it.

He simply asks that I trust him and push through as in James 1:2–4.

> Consider it pure joy, my brothers and sisters, whenever you face trials of many kinds, because you know that the testing of your faith produces perseverance. Let perseverance finish its work so that you may be mature and complete, not lacking anything.

Thank you for reading, and I pray that your road will be prosperous and enjoyed.

— Tom

About the Author

Tom Bloomer has spent over thirty years as a proven sales leader. Having started as an entry-level sales rep, he worked his way up to becoming a Regional VP of Sales responsible for over $40M annually in local ad sales revenues. During his fifteen years as VP of Sales, he worked for three of the leading direct mail advertising companies in the country: Clipper Magazine, Gannett Co. and Valassis Communications. While working in that capacity, he was responsible for strategic growth, change management, company training, and new product sales.

It is this background and wealth of experience that has given Tom the ability to hire, train, coach and lead hundreds of successful people over the years, who have all contributed to his earning the reputation as a tremendous coach and leader.

Tom founded a sales training and consulting company, Bloomer Associates, together with his wife Kelly. They also co-hosted a nationally ranked sales podcast together called "OK Boomer, Teach Me Sales."

As a speaker who motivates and inspires others, Tom enjoys nothing more than presenting his series of sales seminars entitled "Managing Yourself to Success." To learn more about having Tom speak to your sales team, visit emeraldlakebooks.com/bloomer.

Tom and Kelly reside near their adult children in Apex, North Carolina. When not working, they enjoy hiking, movies and long walks with their two dogs, Loki and Lola.

For more great books, please visit us at
emeraldlakebooks.com.